GLASS-FIBRE BOAT REPAIR

James Yates

Helmsman Books

First published in 1992 by
Helmsman Books, an imprint of
The Crowood Press Ltd
Ramsbury, Marlborough
Wiltshire SN8 2HR

British Library Cataloguing in Publication Data

A catalogue record for this book is available from the British Library.

ISBN 1 85223 699 0

Picture Credits
Line-drawings by Claire Upsdale-Jones
Photographs by James Yates

Acknowledgements
The author would like to thank the following for their help in providing information and photographs for this book:

Pat Timoney of Strand Glassfibre (Scott Bader) for help with photographs and permission to reproduce the glossary of terms and other information from their helpful literature; Peter Caplen for technical information; Jim Hurcleson of Osmaster for assistance with the chapter on osmosis; Steve Hunt of Greenacre Photographic; Bernard Martin of Lucas Rists Wiring Systems; Roy Spacey of International Yacht Paints.

To my wife for her inspiration and help

Typeset by Avonset, Midsomer Norton, Bath
Printed in Great Britain by Redwood Press Ltd, Melksham, Wilts

CONTENTS

PREFACE

The object of this book is to give the boat owner enough knowledge to be able to effect repairs to the hull and superstructure of his glass-fibre boat. It will also impart enough information to enable him to care for and maintain the other systems aboard, including the engine, plumbing and toilet. Preventative treatment, done in time, will usually stop a small repair job from becoming a major, time-consuming and ultimately costly one.

The glass-fibre boat has now been around for some thirty-odd years. In its infancy it was hailed as a no-nonsense, maintenance-free material that would last forever! This rather exaggerated statement was soon found to be untrue – glass-fibre boats do need regular maintenance to keep them in tiptop condition. The initial chapters explain what glass fibre is and how it is used in the construction of a boat. Simple mould-making and laminating techniques are fully covered with details of tools required, working conditions and safety aspects. Repair techniques are described for most of the common problems associated with a glass-fibre hull from simple scuffs to the repair of a large hole.

The causes and treatment of osmosis are also explained in a simple and easy to understand way.

Other chapters guide the boat owner through the various maintenance procedures which will ensure that the boat stays reliable and seaworthy. A poorly maintained boat will constantly break down, inconveniencing the owner and even putting his life and that of his crew at risk. Doing your own repair and maintenance work should be part of the total enjoyment of owning a boat; maintenance is an ongoing feature of boating and those who love their boats usually enjoy keeping them in trim, generally saving themselves a good deal of money.

The author has had many years of experience in the care and repair of a wide variety of boats from seagoing cruisers to canal boats and small sailing craft. The knowledge gained over this time is imparted in the clearly written text which is illustrated with many explanatory photographs and diagrams. *Glass-Fibre Boat Repair* should be a book to keep on the boat's bookshelf, next to the toolkit.

1
WHAT IS GLASS FIBRE?

This book will show you how to tackle the basic maintenance to a glass-fibre pleasure boat. It should help you to to reduce boat-yard bills and set you on the right path to deciding just how much care and repair work you would like to do, and be capable of doing on your own craft. To me, tinkering with boats is part of the total pleasure derived from the hobby. Being able to repair a hole in the hull, complete a basic service to the engine or fit an item of equipment brings great rewards, as well as instilling in the owner a better understanding of how the boat and its equipment works. The book will make easy the more tricky aspects of maintenance work which the average boat owner may at first feel he or she is incapable of tackling. So why glass-fibre boats and not wooden boats, aluminium boats or steel boats? The

This Sealine motor cruiser features a hull and superstructure constructed from glass fibre and is a production boat fitted with an inboard engine. Sophisticated mouldings have allowed the designer to produce a good-looking, sporty craft capable of seagoing cruising.

This Flipper sports cruiser features a glass-fibre hull with a cuddy cabin moulded and fitted separately. A canopy covers the rear, open portion of the boat.

answer is one of sheer numbers. By far and away the most prolific type of boat seen afloat around our coastline and on our inland waterways is made from glass fibre, sometimes called glass-reinforced plastic or, in its abbreviated form, GRP.

So, what is glass fibre? Basically, it is a polyester resin that is strengthened by mats or sheets of synthetic fibres known generally as glass, it is extremely malleable, easily formed, relatively easy to work with and when cured has great inherent strength with a good, if not total, resistance to water absorption. The basic component parts of glass fibre are the resin which is a thermo-setting plastic material activated by the addition of a catalyst (an organic peroxide which can be supplied in a powder, putty, liquid or paste form and which cures the resin by a process called exothermics or heat), and the glass, which is a calcium-alumina boro-silicate glass

with an alkali content of less than 1 per cent. In some forms, the resin component requires another constituent called the accelerator which speeds up the curing process, however most of the resins supplied for use in boat building are pre-accelerated. The final component in the equation is the raw GRP matting, or chopped strand mat, a matrix of GRP strands woven into a flexible sheet or mat with varying weave characteristics, which can be rolled up and is easily stored and handled. This, sometimes abbreviated to E Glass, was originally developed for use in electrical insulation systems. It can be supplied in tapes of various widths which are ideal for use as a repair medium or for jointing strips and edging work: chopped strands, of short length, which can be mixed with resin to make a workable mush for the repair of small holes and dents in a hull; woven roving, a thicker, bulkier version of standard matting, and a string-like GRP which is more commonly used on spraying machines in the production of boat hulls and larger mouldings where it is used in conjunction with matting. The range of GRP and resin is quite extensive with types to suit the various stages of boat building and repair.

Characteristics

Each type of glass fibre has its own characteristics and most are used in the construction of the average glass-fibre boat. Standard mat is composed of randomly laid down fibres, compressed together and is bought on rolls, it is capable of absorbing resin easily and, when cured, gives excellent strength and because of its rough nature, good adhesion between each layer. The woven rovings are more like a cloth to look at and come in various grades of thickness and weave. Like matting, rovings readily absorb resin and combine bulk with strength and flexibility of use. Cloth is a smaller grade of woven roving, comprising tightly woven strands. It is strong when cured and very flexible. It is often used in fiddly moulds with lots of tight, sharp corners, and for constructing flat panels. Chopped strand mat (CSM) is principally used by production boat builders and comes in rolls like string. It is fed into special spraying machines that chop the fibres, mix them with the correct proportion of resin, and fire them out at high speed into the mould. A combination of CSM and hand-laid matting is used for the construction of many boat hulls.

Without doubt glass fibre is the most popular of boat-building materials in the pleasure-craft market and is also one of the

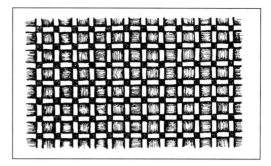

Woven rovings are supplied in a roll and combine strength with good flexibility. They are used as a base from which other layers are built up.

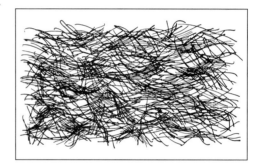

Chopped fibres are usually used in production boat building where they are combined with resin in correct proportions and sprayed on to the work in hand from a special gun.

Chopped strand mat comprises fibres that have been compressed together to form a strong, flexible matting. It is extensively used in the lay-up of a glass-fibre boat.

Polyurethane foam is being sprayed into this hull prior to fitting an interior moulding. Note the substantial strengthening ribs.

easiest to maintain and keep looking smart. An average boat can get away with a couple of waxings and polishes every year, usually once at the start of a season in the spring, the other at the end of the useful cruising season when the boat is being laid up for the long winter months. The only other consideration is a regular coat of an approved antifouling paint on the bottom. General maintenance, as we will see in the following chapters, is relatively simple, with the average DIY boat owner quite capable of completing repair jobs from scratches to punctures in the hull and top sides. Before contemplating any such repairs, it would be sensible for boat owners to familiarize themselves with the general construction

methods used in the completion of their boats.

Basic Construction

The construction of a glass-fibre hull can be divided into two parts: the outer shiny, coloured surface, the part of the boat that goes into the water or the outside of the cabin, called the gel coat, and the layers of glass-fibre matting and resin that make up the thickness of the hull and superstructure, the laminate. Glass-fibre boats are usually built from the outside in. A mould is made to the precise design specification of the craft to be built, the inside of this is first coated with a

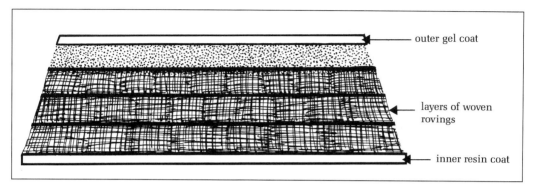

outer gel coat

layers of woven rovings

inner resin coat

This section through an average glass-fibre hull shows the various layers of laminate. First, the outer gel coat, followed by several layers of woven roving and chopped strand mat is finished with an inner resin coating.

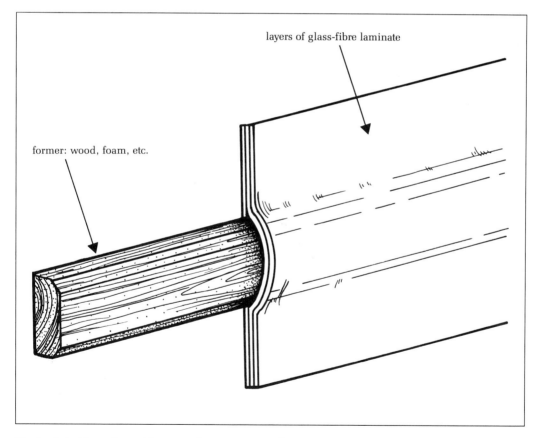

layers of glass-fibre laminate

former: wood, foam, etc.

The top hat stringer is used in areas where extra strength is required. A former is cut to size and is bonded into position inside the hull with several layers of glass-fibre laminate.

9

releasing agent and is then painted with a thin first coat of resin, the gel coat. This coating forms the hard outside skin of the boat and holds the colour pigmentation that will give the boat its aesthetic good looks! On the top of the gel-coat layer upon layer of glass-fibre matting, made up of various weaves, cloths and rovings are laid on and saturated with resin, building up the thickness and binding each layer as they go, in order to form a laminated structure with such a strength to weight ratio that it can exceed even that of steel.

Certain sections of the hull are given even greater strength by using a core construction in which a smaller amount of glass fibre is used to encase timber or foam inserts, or 'cores', finished off with a layer of gel coat. These are glassed into position using more resin and mat to form engine beds, bulkheads, cabin tops and in some cases, even the hull itself. One of the advantages of core construction is that it produces a high strength to weight ratio compared to the same thickness of ordinary laminate. Buoyancy is another factor: foam cores can give extra buoyancy as well as assisting with insulation against heat and noise. Core construction can be slightly more expensive than straight laminating and can, in some circum-stances, be more difficult to repair, depending upon the area affected.

Provided the glass reinforcement has been thoroughly impregnated with resin, the result, after curing, is a cohesive, completely integrated matrix of resin and fibres. This matrix can possess a surprising range of properties, depending upon the type of glass material and the

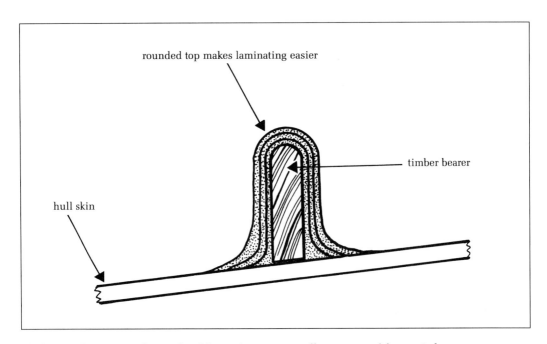

rounded top makes laminating easier

timber bearer

hull skin

The bearers that support the weight of the engines are normally constructed from a timber core, glassed into the bottom of the hull. Rounding the top section of the bearer allows the layers of laminate to flow over the wood in a smooth, uninterrupted manner.

formulation of the resin. In general, the GRP laminate will display excellent tensile and compressive strength, acceptable thermal conductivity, a low coefficient of linear expansion, reasonable chemical resistance and good dielectric properties. Compared to other materials of equivalent strength, it will be light, durable, moisture resistant, non-rusting and economical in use.

Putting it Together

The way in which the various component parts of the glass-fibre boat are put together is an interesting and ingenious process. As we have said, the hull is made up of laminations or layers of glass-fibre matting which have been impregnated and consolidated with resin. A mould is used in this type of construction and the glass-fibre laminations built up or laid up over the top. The mould is usually female and is first coated with a special releasing agent which will allow the finished, cured glass-fibre hull to be easily removed.

The glass-fibre boat is usually put together in two main parts: the hull itself from the gunwhale to the keel and the deck and superstructure. When both these parts have been moulded and cured they are

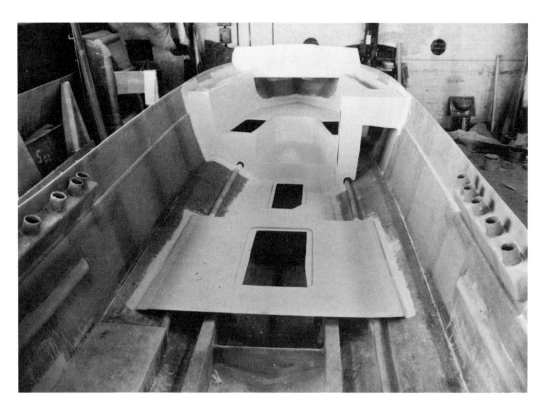

One of the internal mouldings that make up the interior of a modern glass-fibre boat. These might form the shower tray, berths, or galley unit which are constructed separately from the hull and bonded into position before the superstructure is fitted.

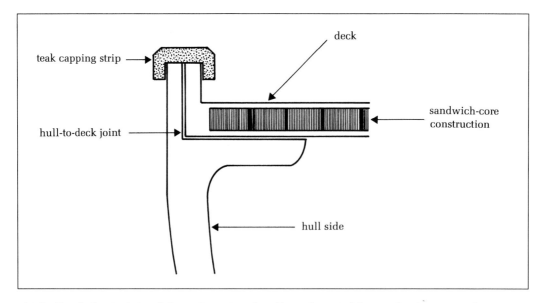

This hull-to-deck joint is bonded together using glass fibre. The top of the joint has been capped with teak for a smart finish. A sandwich core construction gives the boat a lightweight deck with great strength.

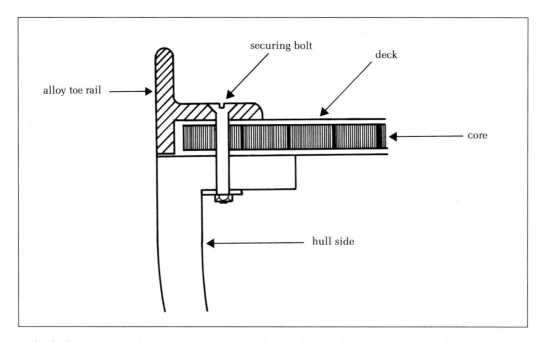

In this hull-to-deck joint the deck is fitted to the hull, sealed with a layer of mastic and is bolted together. A special alloy toe rail disguises the joint.

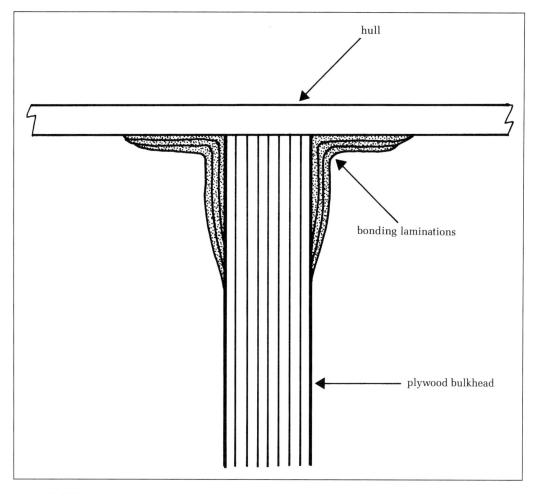

Internal bulkheads, separating cabins and compartments are normally bonded to the hull and superstructure with several layers of glass fibre. This produces an extremely strong joint and helps to give the hull structural strength.

fitted together, bolted and laminated to form a strong single unit. The importance of a good, well-fitted joint between deck and hull is obvious. Strength is built in to the various sections by increasing the 'weight' or number of laminations of glass and resin. This is particularly so near the keel and on decks, and special additives are sometimes added to the resin which increase its hard-wearing properties.

Other forms of strengtheners are ribs and stringers which are moulded in transversely and longitudinally under decks and in the hull. These are usually formed by fitting paper rope or timber strips into position and 'glassing' or bonding them to the main hull using glass-fibre tape or matting. Frames, cabin floors

A completed hull moulding awaiting interior fittings. Engine bearers and part of the cabin floor are already glassed in place.

and bulkheads are usually fitted and laminated into the hull while still in the mould, which allows for accurate alignment and gives them extra rigidity.

Maintenance

Contrary to popular belief, glass-fibre hulls are not maintenance free and, as with most things, regular care will keep the boat looking good and seaworthy for many years to come. If the boat is supplied new, it may only require regular polishing to keep it in trim for several years, but eventually small defects, scratches and day-to-day scuffs will all take their toll and will require some form of remedial repair work. Sometimes this will be a coat of paint, sometimes some simple cosmetic work will have to be done. The following chapters detail the various problems that will be encountered on glass-fibre boats and the step-by-step procedures needed to effect efficient and comprehensive repairs.

SUMMARY

- Glass fibre is a polyester resin that is strengthened by mats or sheets of synthetic fibres known as glass. It is extremely malleable, easily formed, relatively easy to work with and, when cured, has great inherent strength with a good, if not total, resistance to water absorption.

- Certain sections of a boat's hull are given extra strength by using a core construction in which stringers or ribs are glassed into place inside the hull. Formed from wood, cardboard or plastic tube, they are covered with glass-fibre mat and resin and, when cured, form stiffeners in areas of flexibility.

- Glass-fibre boats are **not** maintenance free and regular care will keep the boat looking good and seaworthy for many years.

2
WORKING WITH GLASS FIBRE

The tools required for the care and repair of glass fibre are simple in the extreme. Brushes for laminating, rollers and paddles for consolidating layers of mat and resin, a bottle with graduated cap for the dispensing of catalyst, sturdy scissors for cutting matting and woven rovings, and a cheap polythene bucket for making up mixes are really all that are required for the main jobs of laminating and preparing the glass-fibre components. Brushes can be either cheap paintbrushes or the special glass-fibre laminating brushes bought from chandlers and glass-fibre manufacturers. To these basic tools will be added various scrapers, files, padsaws and craft

resin

glass matting

Using a brush to stipple resin into a piece of glass-fibre matting. Ordinary paintbrushes will do, or you can buy special glass-fibre versions. (Courtesy of Strand Glassfibre.)

knives for the preparation of the work surface and for cutting away damaged portions of the hull. If only small repairs are to be carried out (perhaps the filling in of cracks and small cuts in the gel coat) old plastic squash bottles with the tops removed, wooden spills for stirring resin and a plastic spatula can be employed. Additionally, certain power tools, such as a rotary sander and small jigsaw will be found useful for larger jobs. A small set of scales will also be required for weighing out accurate measures of resin before putting it into the bucket for mixing. Battery-operated metric/imperial scales for kitchen use are ideal and can be bought for only a few pounds.

Some sort of flat surface, such as a folding table will be useful for cutting matting to size and shape and a small electric fan heater to help get the work-place to the desired temperature for glass-fibre working and to start off the curing process will also be a boon.

Literature

One of the first steps when using glass fibre is to get in touch with a reputable manufacturer of glass-fibre products and get them to send you some of their literature on technique and use. Studying this will give you a better insight into the actual application of glass fibre in various areas aboard the boat and will also help in assessing amounts of mat and resin needed for any particular job. Glass-fibre handbooks will, for instance, give you details of the two main types of cold-curing plastics available. The first of these, polyester resin, we have already discussed. It is widely available and is far cheaper than the second type, epoxy resin.

Polyester resins do, in fact, react badly to spilt fuel, with the exception of diesel fuel, and should not be used in the construction of fuel or water tanks. Epoxy resin is mainly used in paint systems and provides excellent adhesion and a sparkling finish.

Safety

Safety aspects should not be overlooked when using glass fibre. The fumes given off from the resin can be quite dangerous, especially when used in confined spaces. Wherever possible, never use resin and catalyst in an enclosed space and always ensure adequate ventilation, using fans if necessary. A suitable set of overalls will be required to protect the clothing while glassing and goggles should be worn to protect the eyes from glass-fibre and resin particles, especially when sanding down or machining laminated panels and moulds. Breathing masks are essential for protecting the nose and mouth when working on or cutting glass fibre, and plastic gloves should always be worn when mixing up resins and when handling glass-fibre matting. Special barrier creams can be bought to spread over the exposed surfaces of the hands and should be rubbed in before laminating or doing any serious mechanical sanding or cutting.

If you suffer from particularly sensitive skin or certain allergies, it would be best to consult your doctor before starting work with glass fibre or its associated products. Once again, remember to work in a well-ventilated area at a temperature around 20° C (68°F) and **do not** smoke or use naked lights or fires in the work area.

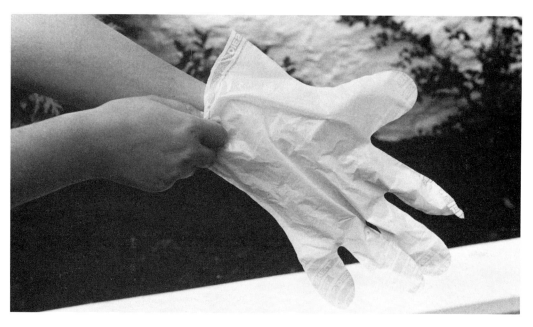

A plentiful supply of plastic gloves should be available to protect hands from resin and fibres.

Male and Female Moulds

The first thing that is required to build a boat in glass fibre is a mould. This is used as a former upon which the layers of glass-fibre laminations are laid up. Some jobs require only a simple mould, flat panels for instance can be produced using nothing more than a piece of thin plywood or hardboard covered with cellophane or Melinex. The basic mould comprises two separate parts: male and female, with the glass fibre being laid up on the outside of a male mould and on the inside of a female one. The finished hull of the boat will have a smooth, shiny surface which will be on the side nearest to the mould, therefore the type of mould used for boat construction will be the female variety. For items requiring a smooth interior surface, for example a shower tray, a sink or some galley mouldings, the male mould will be

the type used. Most solid materials can be used in the construction of a mould from wood and plaster to concrete and metal, the choice being determined by your finished shape and the skill required to build it. However, one of the best materials from which to construct a mould is none other than glass fibre itself.

Making the Plug

The first step in producing a glass-fibre mould is to make a pattern or former, commonly known as a plug, which is an exact mock-up of the finished item. The following description is taken from Strand Glass literature and is reproduced with their permission. The plug can, of course, be an existing example of the real thing, for example a mould for a replacement galley sink unit can be made from another

17

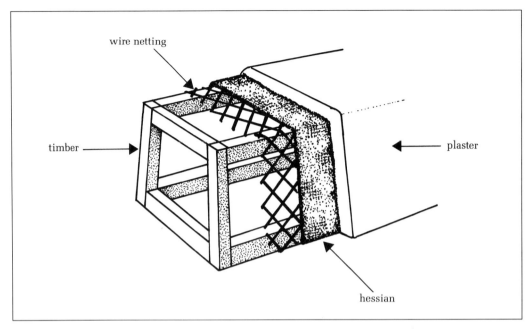

wire netting

timber

plaster

hessian

Typical plug construction using timber, wire netting, hessian and plaster.
(Courtesy of Strand Glassfibre.)

one of the same design. Similarly, a mould for a canoe or dinghy can be taken from an existing boat, although you should be very wary of infringing design copyright. In most cases you will have to build the plug yourself. Almost any materials can be used for this purpose as long as the finished plug is accurate, rigid and has a highly finished surface. Typically, a large plug of the sort needed to produce the mould for a boat would incorporate a rigid wooden framework covered in plywood, hardboard, clay or plaster, reinforced with wire or hessian, or any combination of these.

Whatever material you choose, the surface must be completely smooth and free from blemishes, since the glass-fibre mould will faithfully reproduce any such flaws. Nails should be hammered well in, using a punch; screws should be counter-sunk, and the heads covered with filler. Dents, holes, seams and joints should all be carefully filled. Resin putty is the best filler, although plaster, clay, or even plasticine can be used to good effect. Wooden plugs should be thoroughly sanded down, the grain filled, and covered with several coats of Release Agent No. 1. Alternatively, a final treatment of several coats of Furane resin instead of the release agent, will give a particularly high glaze to the surface which can then be waxed and polished. The Furane should be lightly sanded and polished after each coat. Before using Furane, read the instructions carefully.

Plugs made from plaster or other porous materials should be well sealed with Release Agent No. 1, waxed and polished.

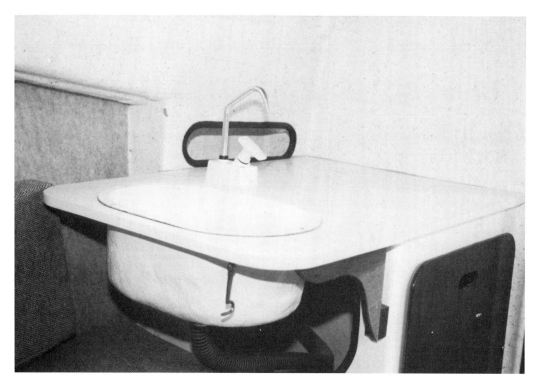

This sink unit has been produced from a small, individual glass-fibre moulding and bonded into the interior of a boat. The cupboard will have been made in a similar way.

Although it demands a great deal of hard work, getting the best possible finish on the surface of the plug will pay dividends at a later stage when the final mould is turned out.

A Basic Glass-Fibre Mould

Before starting to make the mould, treat the finished plug with release agents. Three coats of Release Agent No. 3, followed by one coat of Release Agent No. 2 should suffice, after which the mould itself can be produced by laminating over, or into the plug.

The same method is used as for any other glass-fibre lay-up: a layer of gel coat followed by successive layers of glass mat and general purpose resin. The sequence for laminating can be seen on page 24. The only difference in mould laminating is that the laminations themselves need to be much thicker on a mould than on the finished item. It is easier to remove air pockets if the first layer of mat behind the gel coat is a lightweight one, for example 300g per square metre (10oz per sq. yd). This should be thoroughly consolidated with a metal roller and, if possible, allowed to set before applying the next layer. As a general rule, the mould needs to be twice as thick as the finished item to be made from it. On large moulds, where

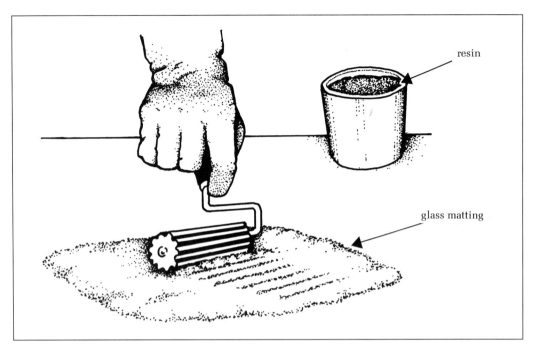

resin

glass matting

A metal roller is used to remove trapped pockets of air and to consolidate the resin into the mat. (Courtesy of Strand Glassfibre.)

this would involve considerable expense, economies can be made by the judicious use of stringers and strengthening ribs. These ribs should be added after the mould has partially cured, otherwise contraction of the laminate around the ribs may leave an impression on the mould surface. The ribs are easily made by laminating over a former of paper rope, polyurethane foam, cardboard or wood. The resulting channel section gives extra rigidity and strength – the former itself does not usually provide any reinforcement.

Split Moulds

If the plug has a deep draught or under-cuts, it will be well nigh impossible to remove the mould unless it is made in two or more sections. This is typically the case on many boat hulls where the mould may be split along the keel line to allow for a slight sloping or 'tumble-home' at the stern. The sections should have flanges about 75mm (3in) wide and at least 50 per cent thicker than the rest of the mould. These flanges can then be drilled to allow the separate sections of the mould to be bolted together.

Leave the mould to cure thoroughly for at least two weeks before removal of the plug, as too early removal can result in distortion. If needed, build a timber framework and bond this on to the mould. Once released from the plug, it is a good idea to drop the mould back on to the plug and allow it to 'breathe' for a couple of

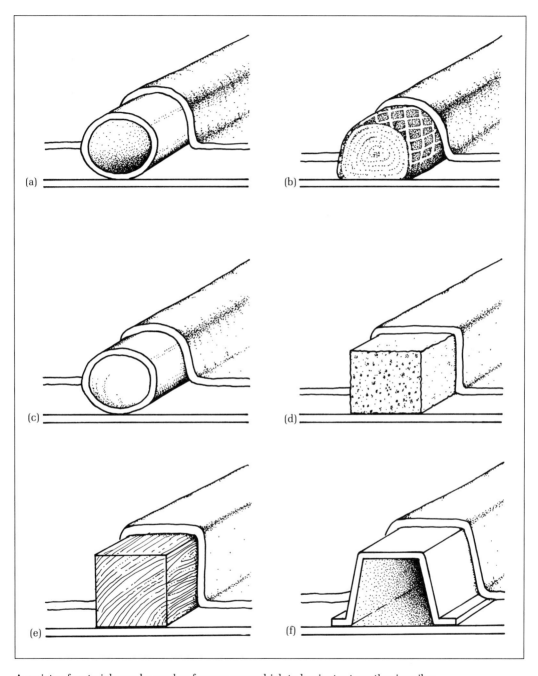

A variety of materials can be used as formers over which to laminate strengthening ribs:
(a) cardboard tube; (b) paper rope; (c) metal tube; (d) foam strip; (e) wood; (f) folded cardboard.
(Courtesy of Strand Glassfibre.)

A complete interior moulding is cleaned up before being fitted inside the hull mould. Note shelves, seats, steps and raised wheelhouse floor are incorporated into this moulding.

Cross-section of part of hull and side deck. The deck is of sandwich construction which gives rigidity combined with light weight, and the deck moulding is bonded to the hull side. A 'V'-shaped rubber fender is bolted through at the joint between deck and hull.

days, after which the surface of the mould can be examined for any imperfections which may require filling or sanding down. Very little of this type of work should be required if the original plug was properly finished. Treat the mould with release agents prior to laminating the finished article. Use between two and six coats of Release Agent No. 3, buffing between each coat and leave at least two hours between each coat to allow it to harden. Finally, apply a coat of Release Agent No. 2. After this has dried, the mould is ready for use.

Section of transom from a high-speed boat. The transom is required to support the outboard engine or sterndrive unit so it must be strongly constructed. A thick layer of glass-fibre laminate is backed by over 2½cm (1in) of plywood.

Basic Laminating Technique

Laminating glass fibre is a relatively simple technique which can be smoothly achieved with a little patience and the right tools. Preparation of the working area is important in order to achieve a dust-free, well-ventilated atmosphere which should be kept at around the 20°C (68°F) mark enabling the curing processes to take place efficiently and properly. Before starting, the mould surface is coated with a release agent which could be a wax polish. This prevents adherence of the gel coat and allows the finished article to be easily separated from the mould after curing. The gel coat itself is brushed or sprayed onto the mould to form the outer skin of the hull, shower tray, sink or whatever is being made, and includes a special pigmentation to give the final colour. The thickness of the gel coat is usually limited to around 400 microns in thickness which gives the hull a certain amount of flexibility and reduces the chances of cracking. Once again, the procedure laid out below is taken from the Strand Glass literature.

Cover the prepared mould surface with a catalyzed gel coat (Resin B) and wait until it has cured to a tacky condition (when it feels slightly sticky, but does not actually adhere to the fingers). Make sure there are no crevices or corners in which the gel coat is still wet, then paint it over with catalyzed general purpose lay-up resin (Resin A). This is much thinner than the gel coat. On to this lay a piece of glass-fibre mat and push it into the wet resin with the brush, using a stippling action. **Do not** paint backwards and forwards as this will cause the glass fibres to separate. More resin can be added at this stage, if

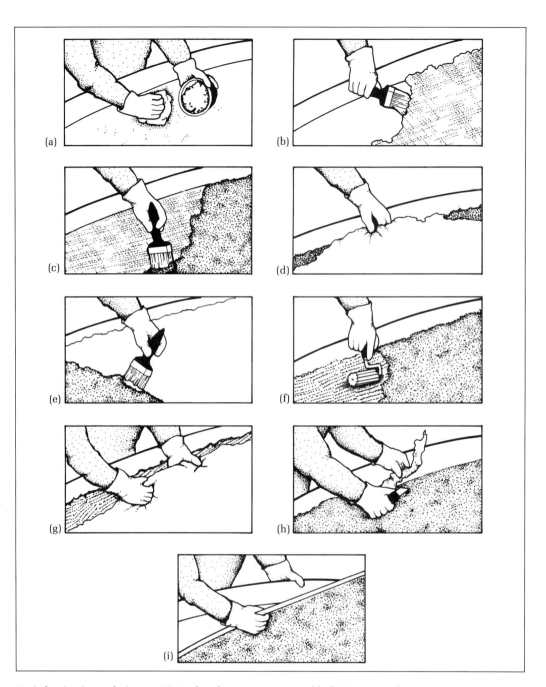

Basic laminating techniques   (a) Apply release agents to mould. (b) Paint on gel coat (Resin B). (c) Paint on lay-up resin (Resin A). (d) Lay down glass-fibre material. (e) Stipple down with brush. (f) Consolidate with metal roller. (g) Add next layer, stipple and consolidate. Repeat for further layers. (h) Trim off rough edges when cured. (i) Release finished item from mould. (All diagrams are courtesy of Strand Glassfibre.)

necessary, to ensure that the glass-fibre material is fully impregnated. When the mat is completely wetted through, the layer should be rollered with a metal laminating roller to force out air bubbles and consolidate the resin/glass matrix.

Once consolidated, a further coat of catalyzed Resin A and another layer of mat can be added, and the process repeated. Any number of layers can be built up, depending upon the thickness and strength required. For many jobs, only two layers will be needed, but for large hulls, sometimes up to ten or more layers will be required, especially in areas requiring great strength, such as the keel and bow section. It will not be necessary to wait for each layer of mat/resin to set hard before applying the next, provided not more than two or three layers are built up at the same time.

Clean Tools

Whilst laminating, the resin on the brushes and other tools will begin to cure and, if left, will eventually set hard. To prevent this, the tools should be soaked in acetone or brush cleaner which will dissolve the resin. You should remember that acetone is highly inflammable so **do not** smoke or use naked flames in the work area. All brushes and rollers should be dry before use.

Stiffening

A thin laminate can be made much stronger or more rigid by adding stiffeners in the form of ribs or box sections. These are easily produced by laminating over formers of paper rope, polyurethane foam or even cardboard or wood. In boat building stringers are built into a hull at certain points for strengthening, especially in areas which have a high flexibility. An average stringer can be made by using a foam or timber former fitted to the inside of the hull, which is then laminated over with several layers of chopped strand mat of cloth. These are sometimes called top-hat strengtheners because of the shape of the laminate formed over them.

Finishing

Normally, a glass-fibre laminate will have a smooth surface (that nearest the mould) and a rough surface. The rough surface can be given a more acceptable finish by adding a layer of surface tissue or woven glass fibre which must be applied whilst the laminate is still wet. When all the necessary layers have been built up, the laminate should be left to cure. Rough edges can be trimmed off with a craft knife when the laminate has reached the 'green' stage, i.e. has started to go hard. Once fully hardened, trimming will require a hacksaw with a metal cutting blade. Remember to wear a breathing mask and goggles when cutting or machining glass fibre.

When fully cured, the moulding can be released from the mould. If this proves difficult, due to a complex mould shape or insufficient use of release agents, the moulding can sometimes be sprung out by striking the mould with the flat of the hand. **Do not** use a hammer for this job, since this will probably crack both mould and moulding! A rubber mallet can be used, but requires some skill. Wooden or plastic wedges (but not metal) can also be used to release a difficult moulding, although great care must be taken not to scratch the laminate or mould.

Moulding Engine Beds

If buying a bare hull to fit out, or replacing an original engine with a new model, the engine beds will have to be fitted or renewed. As this is an ideal example of simple glassing techniques, it is appropriate to describe the procedure used in this chapter. Most other glass-fibre work is carried out in the same way. These are the two sturdy supports which are bonded to the inside of the hull bottom on to which the engine mounting feet and the engine itself are fitted. The engine beds themselves need to be particularly strong as they will be taking the weight of the engine and will be required to provide both rigidity and support. Many boats use steel engine beds but timber ones are just as popular and probably easier for the DIY boat owner to construct and fit.

Before any construction work can be carried out, the plans of the boat should be studied. When buying a bare hull to fit out, companies who supply hulls and superstructures, such as Colvic Craft, will supply detailed sets of drawings from which measurements and stress details can be taken. These drawings are required in order to ascertain the angle of the

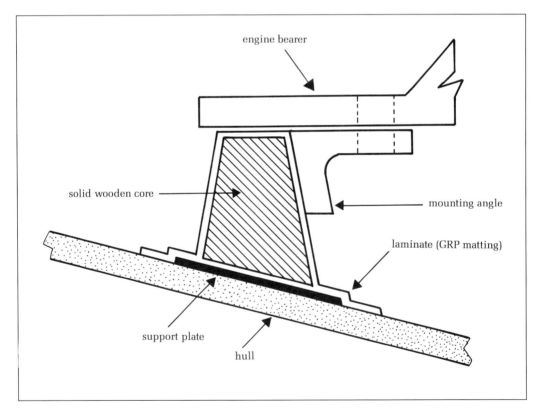

Detail of engine bearer showing supporting plate, timber core and glass-fibre laminations securing the bearer to the hull. The mounting foot attached to the engine block can be seen at the top.

propeller shaft which usually follows the angle of the engine beds themselves.

String Line

The propeller shaft angle can be visually reproduced by constructing a simple wooden frame outside the hull at the transom, tying on a string line, and using the drawings, measuring down from the bottom of the hull at a point where the shaft will be fitted and extending this line forward inside the boat to secure it at the most convenient point. The hole in the hull where the string passes through should be made large enough to allow it to run in a perfectly straight line from the framework aft to the inboard securing point.

With this line in position it should now be possible to check the angle and depth of the shaft supporting 'P' brackets at their mounting positions below the hull and then calculate the angle of the engine beds at the point at which they will be bonded into position. The ease at which this will be achieved will largely depend upon the comprehensiveness of the supplied drawings.

Engine Mock-Up

A simple mock-up of the engine should now be made from scrap timber which incorporates the exact positions of the engine mounting feet in conjunction with the height above them of the gearbox output shaft. This simple assembly will ensure that the height of the top face of the engine beds will be correct when the

A simple mock-up of the engine is made from scrap timber which incorporates the exact positions of the engine mounting feet and the height above them of the gearbox output shaft.

The timber baulks that will form the engine bearers are cut to size and fitted into position.
The bed at the bottom of the picture has been set on to a cement/resin base.

engine is lowered into place. It can also be used to check that there is sufficient clearance above the hull bottom for the engine, which is dictated by the sump. It is, in fact, the sump clearance that will decide how far forward the engine will sit on its beds. The further forward they are, the higher they will be.

The next stage is to select the timber required for the beds. This can be scrap baulks of reclaimed timber, if necessary, as long as they are in good, sound condition with few holes and no rotten sections. Once the correct bed angle has been ascertained from the string line there should be no problems in cutting the timber to the correct length and shape. Once the timber has been cut to size it will be time to start glassing the individual pieces into position in the hull.

Ventilation

As you will be working in a relatively small area with little ventilation it will be important to make proper preparations before opening the resin and commencing on the actual glassing work. Try and set up some form of fresh air circulation: a large extractor fan would do the job, set up on the deck with a length of trunking extending down into the compartment to

After cutting a piece of chopped strand mat to size it is bonded into place by applying resin from a brush, using a stippling action.

ensure that the resin fumes are constantly removed. A plentiful supply of cheap plastic gloves should be available to protect hands from the catalyzed resin, and set up some sort of table or flat surface to allow the roll of chopped strand mat to unroll as required for cutting off to length.

With these preparations made you can now start glassing. The first job is to cut some lengths of glass mat of the appropriate length for the job ready to use. If larger areas than can be conveniently handled in single pieces are to be glassed, it is better to tear the mat rather than cutting it as this thins the edge down so that the two overlapping pieces are of the same thickness as the rest of the lay-up. For a job requiring smaller-shaped pieces it is more convenient and quicker to cut the mat with a craft knife. The mixing of the resin and catalyst is straightforward by

volume using the cap of the catalyst bottle as the measure, but it is essential to stir the mixture extremely well otherwise the cured resin/mat could be low on strength and might eventually fail.

Stippling Action

With a piece of pre-cut mat placed into position, brush on a generous amount of resin and work it swiftly through the mat, using a stippling action to ensure that every fibre is well soaked. The brush can be used to work the mat right into the corners and to ensure that no air is trapped within the lay-up. After this has been done, a roller is used on the flat, open areas to consolidate the mat and remove any last traces of air. The next piece of mat can then be laid in place, overlapping the edge of the first piece and the same process

Several more layers of glass fibre will be required here before the job is complete. Both engine beds have been bonded into position to form a sturdy structure integral with the hull.

repeated until the entire engine bed is covered with one layer of mat and resin. Before the first layer is completely cured a second layer should be applied, followed by three more layers which should then be left undisturbed to cure hard for several days before any weight is applied to them.

With the beds built and bonded into place the next job will be to lower the engines into position and to see whether your initial calculations for the engine beds were correct!

Finally, it is worth mentioning once again a few points of safety when working with glass fibre and resins. Always work in a well ventilated area, wear protective gloves when mixing resin and catalyst, use goggles to cover the eyes and a mask to prevent dust when cutting, filing or sanding down any glass-fibre product.

The engine, finally fitted into position on the new engine beds and bolted down on its mounting feet.

This boat, ravaged by a fire, looks almost a right-off, but damage seems to have been confined to the wheelhouse and down one side. It should be possible to cut away badly damaged areas and effect repairs. However, it might be prudent to obtain a surveyors report before starting work.

SUMMARY

- Before starting work on your boat, contact a reputable manufacturer of glass-fibre products. He will be a mine of information on working with the material, often supplying specification sheets and other helpful literature.

- Laminating with glass fibre is a relatively simple technique, but remember to work in a well-ventilated area, wear rubber gloves to protect the hands, and goggles when finishing or cutting cured glass fibre.

- Once you have finished laminating, your tools will require cleaning. Soaking them in acetate or brush cleaner which will dissolve the resin is a good tip, and because this is a flammable material, never use naked flames in the workplace.

- Resin is usually best applied to matting with a brush using a stippling action. In this way, air bubbles are purged from the work and the fibre-glass mat receives its full quota of resin.

3
GENERAL REPAIRS

Sometimes a new boat will be delivered from the manufacturer with many small flaws in the hull and topside surfaces. Some of these flaws may be visible, some not so easy to see. All will need some form of attention at some time in the boat's life, in addition to the run of the mill scratches, dents and accidents that occur during normal use. The flaws that occur during the manufacturing process can be brought on by several reasons. If the gel-coat mixture is incorrect, too thick or too thinly applied, or if it is not allowed its proper curing time at the correct temperature, small blisters, hairline cracks and pin holes will appear in the surface coating in the early months after the boat is launched. These and other blemishes, scuffs and scratches should be attended to before they become worse, allowing water to seep or wick into the laminate, causing all sorts of problems which could be expensive and time consuming to rectify.

You might at first assume that the care and maintenance of a glass-fibre boat will be just as difficult as that of a wooden one, but careful examination of the hull for surface blemishes every so often during the cruising season and thoroughly at laying-up time will soon give the owner enough experience to spot potential areas of trouble and take the necessary action to effect repairs. Starting at the bows of the boat and working slowly towards the stern, carefully examine all the deck fittings: cleats, fairleads, stem-head rollers and sea railings for security and rigidity. Some of these fittings, especially cleats, are required to take quite hefty loads and need to be well bedded down and bolted through the deck to solid metal backing plates. Tell-tale signs of looseness and stress will show up in crazing or splits in the glass fibre emanating from the bolts holding the fitting down. Other areas to watch out for are the section of coachroof

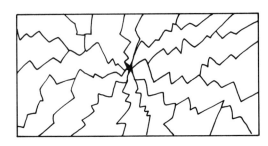

Random crazing of the gel-coat layer caused by a collision, or weight being dropped, but not penetrating through to the laminate.

A starcrack which has been caused by impact or stress. Cracks radiate out from the centre of damage.

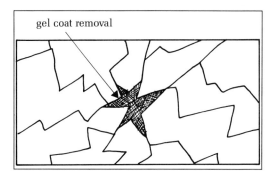

gel coat removal

Close up at the centre of a starcrack showing gel coat removal. Cracks at this point may be deeper than at the edges of the 'star'.

at the bottom of the mast where similar signs of stress might indicate that the main mast supports below deck need attention.

Points at which stays and rigging are attached should be checked in a similar way, especially if over-tensioning is suspected.

Cracks and Scratches

Let us now look at the various types of damage and how they can be rectified. Cracks and scratches can sometimes be difficult to tell apart, especially if they are of the hairline variety. Scratches are part of the normal wear and tear on a glass-fibre boat and, as long as they are not too deep, should not be the cause of too much worry. Minor scratches can usually be buffed out using glass-fibre polish but, if they are

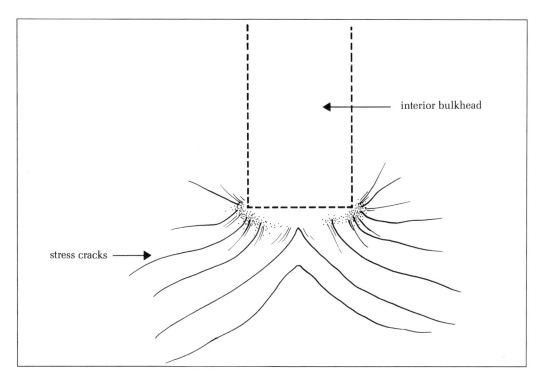

interior bulkhead

stress cracks

Stress cracks caused by internal bulkhead movement. Cracks can be seen radiating from the site of the bulkhead. Look behind for causes.

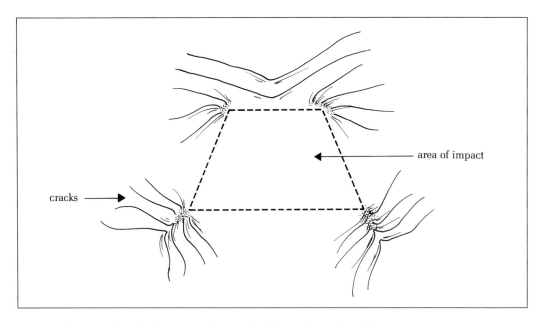

Stress cracks caused by a hard object striking the hull from the inside and leaving an impression similar in shape to the object.

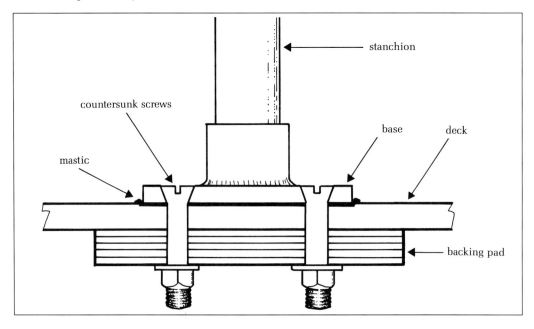

Deck fittings require sturdy backing pads to prevent flexing and distortion of the glass-fibre deck. This stanchion base has been bolted through to a thick piece of plywood after being bedded down on to a special sealing mastic.

These cracks have been caused by a heavy weight being dropped on to the side decks of this boat.

deeper, sanding down the edges followed by a polish with glass-fibre polishing compound will clear them. Cracks can be more difficult to treat. First, widen the crack using a sharp knife or drill and V-shaped grinding burr to allow it to hold the special gel-coat putty and try to extend the cut a little beyond the crack at both ends to help avoid a build-up of stress when the repair has cured. Remove all debris and dust from the crack with a small paint brush, wearing gloves to protect the hands from tiny shards of glass and a face mask to stop dust. Clean the surrounding area of wax, grease or grime which may prevent the adherence of the putty, but avoid the use of glasspaper or abrasive solvents which could make the problem worse. Once the crack is clean, mix enough gel-coat putty to complete the job, working it into the crack and building up the layers with a flexible-bladed putty knife. Work the putty well into the crack, ensuring no air is trapped behind and leave a small amount protruding to allow for any shrinkage.

To help the gel coat cure completely, the area of damage should be covered with a small piece of cellophane or plastic sheet, taped firmly down on all sides. The manufacturer's advice on curing temperatures should be followed, but in the event of the air temperature being below about 13°C (55°F) (quite possible in the UK) place a small heat lamp near the crack for about 20 minutes which will start the curing process. Remove the lamp after this time. After the putty has partially cured to a still tacky state, remove the cellophane and carefully slice away any putty protruding above the level surface using a sharp craft-knife blade. Once fully hardened, buff the area using a fine surface-cutting compound or a very fine

35

scuffing

Simple scuffing and slight surface abrasions can usually be cleaned and polished out, finally buffing up to the original shine.

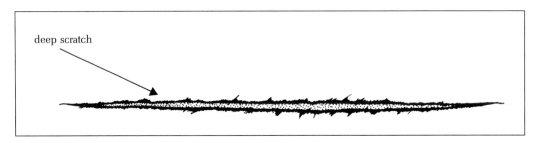

deep scratch

Deeper scratches like this will require a full repair job as the gel coat has been penetrated through to the laminate. Failure to do so will allow water to seep in causing other, more serious long-term damage.

grade of wet-and-dry glasspaper. Finish with a coating of glass-fibre wax.

Severe Dents

If the boat has received a severe bash, say from an anchor being dropped on to the deck or by hitting the corner of a pontoon when coming in to moor in the wind, the damage might have penetrated through the gel coat and back into the first few layers of matting. All the damaged laminate should be cut back and removed. In some bad cases this might mean making a hole right through the hull. The edges of the hole should be filed flat and smooth using a coarse file, followed by a finer one, then glasspaper. The area around the hole should be roughened to give a key to the new gel coat and laminations; the gel coat should be undercut at an angle. Once the hole has been prepared, it can be filled with glass-fibre paste to within about 3mm (⅛in) of the surface. Once the paste has cured, mix the gel coat with hardener as recommended and press it well into the hole, ensuring that it is pushed into the prepared undercut. Leave the gel coat slightly proud, then cover the patch with some cellophane or a sheet of Melinex, rolling out any trapped air bubbles with a

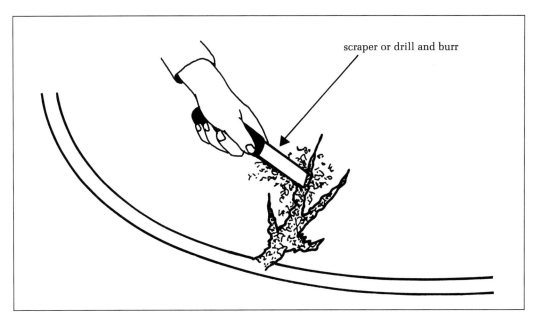

scraper or drill and burr

(a) Use a V-shaped burr on a drill or a scraper to cut back the crack to allow the epoxy putty to be inserted.

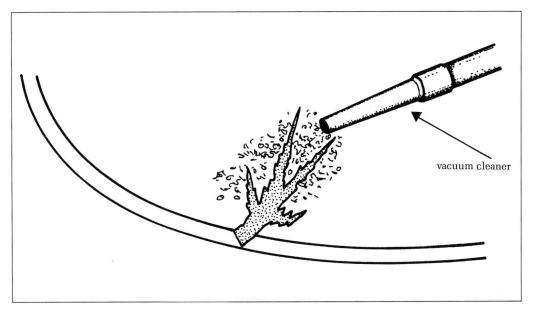

vacuum cleaner

(b) Use a vacuum cleaner to suck up debris, then clean off surface dirt or wax which could prevent the putty from adhering to the surface.

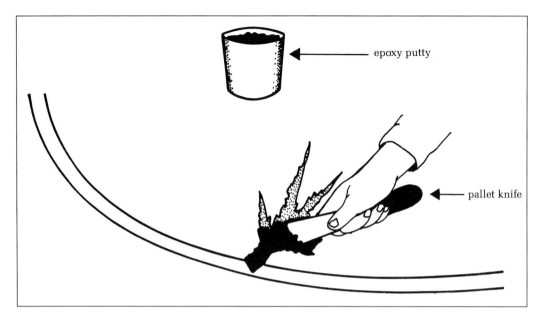

(c) Insert the epoxy putty using a flexible-blade putty knife, allowing a small amount to protrude above the surface level.

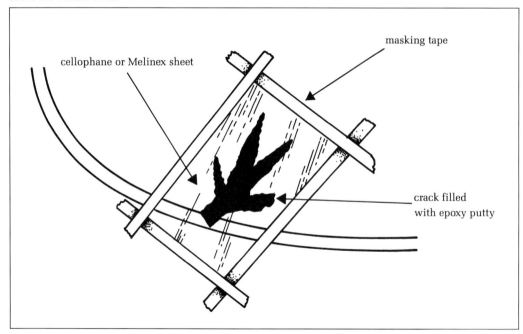

(d) Cover the area with a sheet of Melinex or cellophane, rolling out any trapped air with a metal tube or roller. Tape the edges down firmly with masking tape.

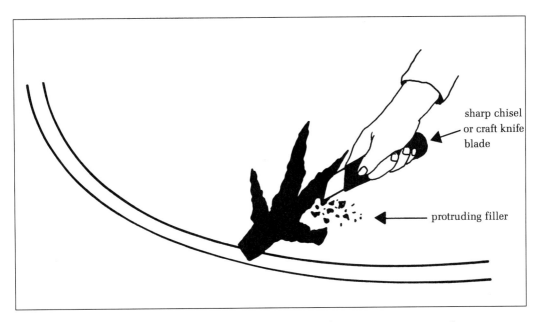

sharp chisel or craft knife blade

protruding filler

(e) When cured to a tacky consistency, remove the cellophane and scrape any excess putty from the crack, using a sharp chisel or craft-knife blade.

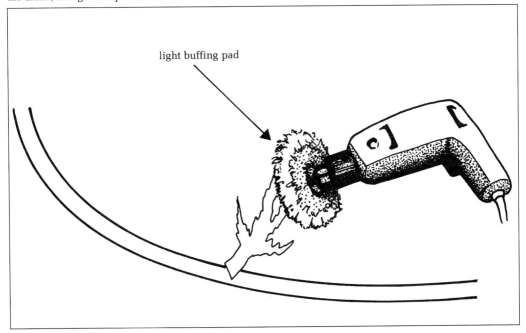

light buffing pad

(f) Finish the repair by polishing the repaired crack with a power drill, buffing pad and a fine grade of polishing powder.

These holes have been caused by the boat falling on to a quayside mooring bollard after slipping on its sling while being off-loaded from a low-loader by crane. The inner layers of laminate have been pushed back, tearing through the woven rovings. Note the impact fractures at the top of the hole. Before a patch can be fitted the whole of the damaged area will need to be cut out and the edges filed smooth.

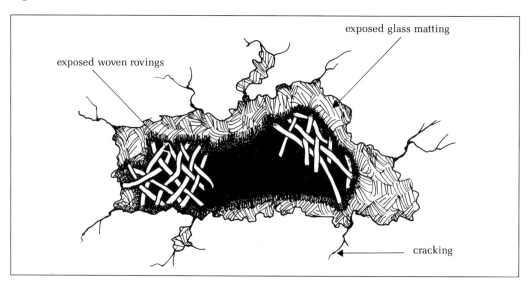

exposed glass matting

exposed woven rovings

cracking

A major hole through the hull. Here there is a puncture through the gel coat and all layers of laminate. It might look serious but can be repaired by the DIY boat owner!

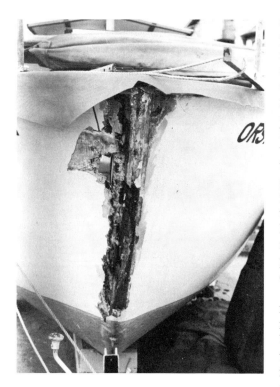

Damage such as this has been caused by a severe collision at the bows and has exposed the timber stem post. The area will require cutting back to sound material before repairs can be undertaken.

small metal tube. Once cured, the repair can be finished in the usual way.

Delamination

Another problem, although less common than scratches, dents and cuts, is delamination where the layers of glass-fibre matting and resin peel away from each other. This can be caused by water seepage, poor laying-up techniques or localized damage that has been allowed to get bigger until whole areas of gel coat and mat start to come away from the hull.

Certain areas of the hull and deck are more prone to delamination than others, for instance on deck at the point where people climb aboard and regular heavy footfalls and scrambling take place, or at the foredeck which takes a regular hammering during lowering and raising anchor. The bow area near the water is also very vulnerable to delamination because it takes regular knocks from quays, lock gates and floating debris which can impact at great force in a boat travelling through the water at high speed. Delamination should be repaired immediately if it is to be contained and to prevent water ingress into the bare, exposed fibre matting.

The repair should be started by removing all damaged and frayed matting, resin and gel coat in the immediate area. Use a sharp chisel and wooden mallet for this job, clearing away dust and loose fibres until sound laminate is reached. An area of about 15cm (6in) around the damage should be sanded down using an electric drill and medium-grade sanding disc. This will key the area and help the fresh matting and resin to adhere properly. Ensure that all dust is cleared away, washing down the sanded area with a mild solution of soapy water.

Taking a piece of chopped strand glass-fibre matting, cut a piece to a size enough to cover the area of damage, then soak with resin, stippling down with a resin or paint brush, working out all trapped air and ensuring a tight, overall fit. It will be easier to match the contours of the hull if small slits are cut into the edges of the mat with a pair of scissors before starting. Consolidate the laminate with a special roller and build up the layers of laminate until the new patch is almost flush with the hull surface, after which it can be left

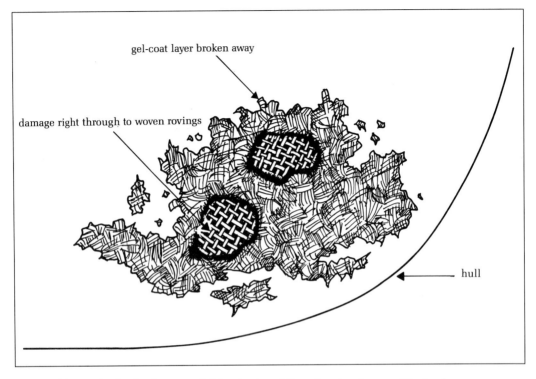

gel-coat layer broken away

damage right through to woven rovings

hull

A severe blow at the forefoot has caused delamination of the gel coat and some of the top layers of laminate. Damage in this area should be repaired without delay as the effect of water rushing past will accelerate the problem by loosening and peeling away more gel coat.

to cure. Cover the matting with two or three pieces of glass-fibre cloth to give the repair strength, then sand down the edges to match the original surface, finishing with primer and an epoxy paint system of your choice.

Puncture Repairs

Occasionally the hull itself may become punctured, all layers of laminate being holed right through the hull thickness. This can happen accidentally by other craft hitting the boat or by striking projections on the dock wall when coming in to moor. The damage can at first seem disastrous, but holes up to about 30cm (1ft) in diameter can be successfully repaired by the owner. One of the most important points to consider when tackling a repair to a hole is to begin the work as soon as possible. If damage caused at the end of the season is left throughout the winter, damp and frost will make the problem very much worse. To make an effective repair the boat needs to be ashore where the area of damage can dry out thoroughly and where work can be carried out in comparative comfort.

Even large areas of damage should not provide any problems to the DIY owner as long as they are flat or on a single curve. Multiple curves and very complex sections are obviously more of a problem and require more complicated working, but are still within the scope of the amateur. For the very best appearance and the strongest job it is essential to have access to the inside of the damaged area so as to be able to work from both inside and out.

The first task is to cut back the damaged area to sound material to give a firm base for the repair to adhere to. The edges should then be chamfered either inside or out, depending on which method of repair is chosen. The inside area surrounding the damage must be roughened to ensure good adhesion and this can be performed with a coarse sanding disc in a drill or an angle grinder.

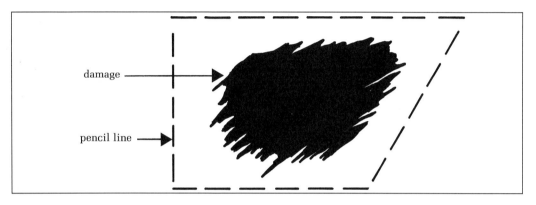

(a) Mark around the damaged area with a pencil and ruler.

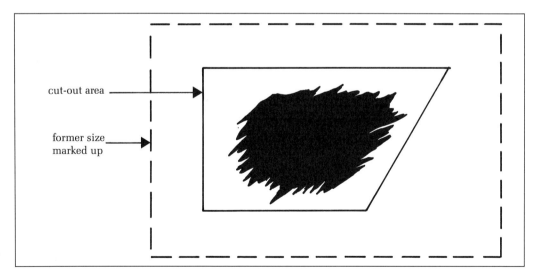

(b) Cut away the area of damage with a padsaw or jigsaw, then mark the size of hardboard former required.

The most professional job is achieved by performing the repair in the same way that the boat was built by laying up the new skin from the inside, and for this type of repair the chamfer must be towards the inside.

Using a Former

A piece of hardboard should be cut to a size which overlaps the damaged area all round, and which will form the face of the mould on to which the new skin of glass fibre will be laid up. The flat face of the hardboard should be covered with a sheet of Melinex which is a resin-proof polythene-type sheet available from Strand Glass. If you cannot obtain this, a sheet of thickish cellophane can be substituted. The Melinex must be perfectly smooth on the face of the hardboard otherwise any ripples or creases will show up on the finished skin of the boat. The board is then offered up over the hole and secured tightly in place using a strong adhesive tape or small self-tapping screws. If the area being repaired is on a

curve, check from inside the boat that the Melinex sheet is still perfectly flat against the board when fixed into place against the contour of the hull. It is also essential that the board is pressed tightly against the edge of the hole all round otherwise the join between old and new glass fibre will not be perfectly smooth.

Disposable gloves should be worn to protect the hands before mixing the resin and it is also important to choose a warm, dry day. The first step is to mix a quantity of gel-coat resin and catalyst to the proportions stated in the instructions. If it is proposed to match the gel coat with the original colour of the hull, this must be done by adding the appropriate pigment to the gel coat resin after mixing in the catalyst.

Area of Damage

Roughly work out the area of damage and mix sufficient to do the job in one coat; 500g (1lb) of gel coat will cover an area of approximately 56 square metres (67 sq. yds). Paint the surface of the Melinex

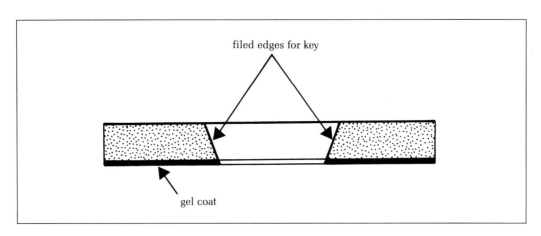

(c) File back the edges of the gap at an angle to provide a good key for the new gel coat and laminate.

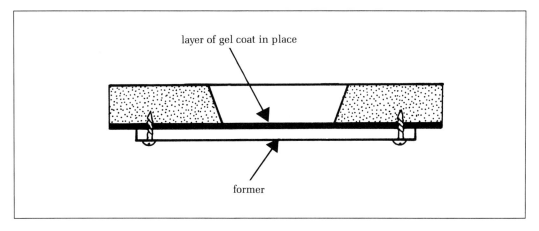

layer of gel coat in place

former

(d) Screw the former into position after covering it with a sheet of Melinex or cellophane sheeting. The gel coat can now be painted in, making sure that it is tucked right into the cut-back portion.

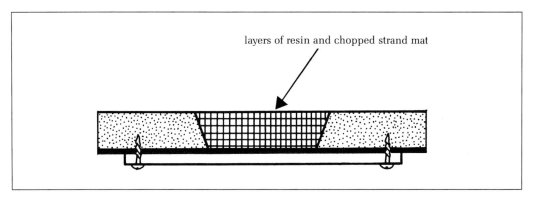

layers of resin and chopped strand mat

(e) The first few layers of matting are glassed into position inside the hole.

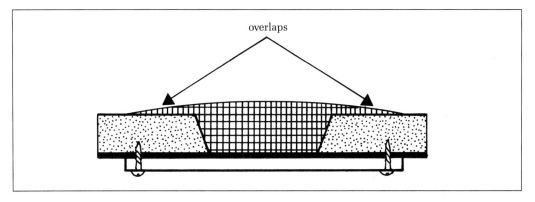

overlaps

(f) The final layers of matting are built up to form an overlap either side of the hole to give the repair strength. Once these have cured, the former can be removed and the repair finished as usual.

sheet with the gel coat, ensuring that it covers right to the edges of the hole. Paint over the edges as well and then leave it to harden. This should take around one-and-a-half hours at 20°C (68°F) and longer in cooler weather. When it is ready it will feel slightly tacky but will not stick to the fingers.

Mix up a quantity of lay-up resin 'A' and apply a generous coat to the gel coated Melinex and the surrounding area, then lay a piece of medium-weight chopped strand mat, large enough to overlap the repair all round on to the resin, and stipple it well into place with the brush, ensuring that it goes right into the edges between the hull skin and the Melinex; then use a roller to remove any air bubbles and ensure that the mat is properly wetted through with resin. When properly wetted, the mat becomes translucent and individual strands can no longer be seen. Repeat this procedure with subsequent layers of mat, each overlapping the previous layer until the thickness of the repair equals that of the original hull skin.

At this stage the repair can be left to harden which will take at least two hours at 20°C (68°F). When properly hardened the Melinex sheet can be peeled off and any indentations found in the gel coat layer filled with further gel coat, covered with Melinex and left to harden. The repaired area should then be left to cure for a week. The final job, if the gel coat match was precise, is to rub down the repair with wet-and-dry paper until perfectly smooth and finish off by polishing with rubbing compound, or for painting, just rub down smooth.

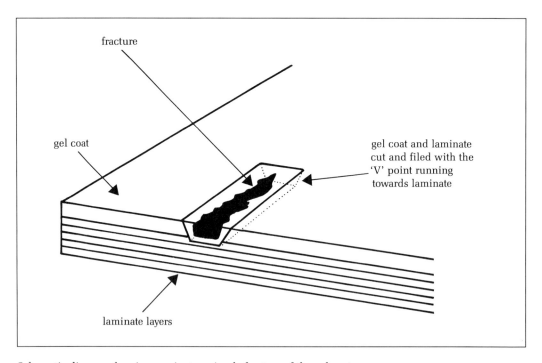

fracture

gel coat

gel coat and laminate cut and filed with the 'V' point running towards laminate

laminate layers

Schematic diagram showing repairs to a simple fracture of the gel coat.

Repairing a Hole from the Outside

It is possible to make repairs to holes from the outside only, but this a very inferior method compared with working from both sides and should only be employed where strength is not an important factor to the job. Once again, the hole must be trimmed back to sound material and the edges chamfered, this time towards the outside, and the inside surrounding area cleaned up as well as possible by hand using a coarse grade of glasspaper. Perforated zinc, available from motor accessory shops or glass-fibre manufacturers, is cut to size to overlap the hole all round by about 5cm (2in). Five pieces of mat of the same size should also be cut. Lay the zinc on a clean surface or a piece of Melinex and paint it with Resin 'A', following this with a layer of mat. Stipple the mat with the brush to ensure that it is fully wetted out and then run over it with the roller to remove any air. Repeat this procedure rapidly until all five pieces of mat have been applied.

Working quickly to prevent the resin hardening before completion, bend a piece of stiff wire (such as a wire coat hanger) into a U-shape and push it through the centre of the zinc/mat patch (from the zinc side). The patch is then carefully inserted through the hole and pulled up against the inner surround of the hole using the wires. Use a batten and spacers to attach the wires to hold the patch in place while it hardens. After-

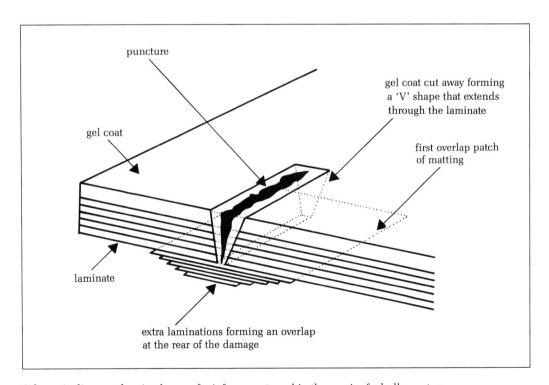

puncture

gel coat cut away forming a 'V' shape that extends through the laminate

gel coat

first overlap patch of matting

laminate

extra laminations forming an overlap at the rear of the damage

Schematic diagram showing layers of reinforcement used in the repair of a hull puncture.

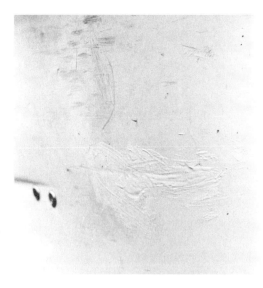

An example of a botched repair to a deep scratch in the hull. Some filling compound has been used and has been painted over without any rubbing down or finishing. This will knock the price down when the boat is being sold.

wards, remove the wire, batten and spacers and fill up the area to just below the surface using a paste of catalyzed Resin 'A' and shredded chopped strand mat. When this has hardened, apply gel-coat resin painted on and taped over with Melinex. Leave to cure for a week; finish off by rubbing down and either painting or polishing.

Repairing Scratches

Scratches can be simply repaired, the action needed depending upon the depth and length of each scratch. Slight scratches which can hardly be seen, except on a light-coloured hull, can normally be removed by rubbing down with a fine grade of paper or a grinding compound and burnishing with a special

Small scuffs and minor abrasions can usually be polished out using a gentle buffing compound.

glass-fibre polishing paste. Deeper scratches must first be cleaned out using acetone which acts as a degreaser. Apply this with a soft cloth and remember to use only the minimum amount necessary as too much will start to attack the gel coat causing more problems than if the scratch had been left alone. Once clean, the scratch can be filled with fresh gel coat, not forgetting to seal it off from the air with cellophane to allow complete curing. Leave the filler slightly proud of the hull surface and finish by rubbing down with fine wet-and-dry paper, burnishing as before.

Repairing Deck Fittings

Loose or broken cleats, fairleads and rigging anchor points can be dangerous, causing boats to break free of their moorings and equipment prone to failure,

Certain deck fittings, like this mooring bollard, are required to take great loading and strain. They should be securely fitted, bedding down on waterproof sealant and bolted through to backing pads of metal or plywood.

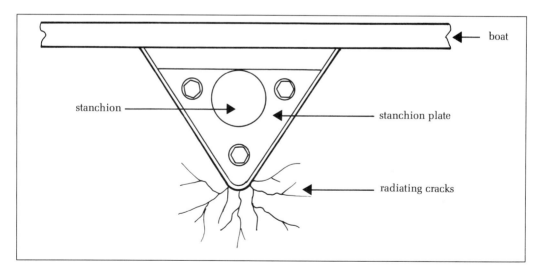

Stress crack in the deck of a boat caused by excess strain being placed on a fitting, in this case a stanchion tube which is often used as a grab rail to pull on when boarding. This puts great strain on the stanchion base which, if not properly secured, will eventually work loose and pull right out of the deck. The stress crack is the first sign of something going wrong.

Sea rails and their support stanchions take tremendous strain because they are often used as grab handles when getting aboard. The area of the deck around their bases should be checked for signs of cracking which could mean that the fitting is becoming loose.

Using a portable electric drill, with screwdriver bit, to tighten the screws at the bottom of a stanchion base.

One of the best ways of protecting the hull of a glass-fibre boat is to give the surface a regular coating of glass-fibre wax polish.

usually at the most inconvenient time. The reason for this can be due to water seeping under the fitting and rotting through the timber below, the bolts themselves becoming loose, or simply that so much load has been placed on the fitting that the surrounding glass fibre has become weakened to an extent that the first puff of wind snaps the cleat out through the deck, bolts and all.

Problems such as this usually occur on older boats, so if buying second-hand always check on the security of deck fittings by giving them a good sharp tug with your hands. This goes for cleats, anchor winches, sea rails and mooring bollards and should be done during your pre-purchase inspection.

The main rules for fitting deck and skin gear are that the main load-bearing ones such as cleats and winches are solidly bolted through the deck to strong backing plates or pads and that the bolt holes are saturated in a good quality waterproof sealant such as Life Caulk. On glass-fibre boats it is easy to increase the thickness of the deck with extra layers of matting and this, with a large metal backing plate, should give the fitting the strength required.

If the deck is a sandwich construction for example, with two or more layers of laminate with a balsa or foam-filled centre section, the problem changes as over-tightening the fitting could result in the laminate becoming crushed and mal-formed. This can be overcome by fitting metal collars around the bolts to bush them out and take the strain.

Smaller fittings, such as fender eyes, are usually screwed straight down to the deck. Care should be taken to ensure the correct type of screws are used. Ordinary wood screws are useless and will strip out immediately upon being tightened, especially when screwing into glass fibre. Use stainless steel self-tappers into a previously drilled pilot hole or, better still, bolts. Remember that round-headed screws are better than countersunk ones as

the thickness of the glass fibre may not be enough to accommodate the countersunk depth of the screwhead.

Replacement Windows

The small slit-type perspex windows so often seen on smaller boats can easily become cracked or broken and the only way out is complete replacement. Some windows can only be fitted by using the correct manufacturer's replacement type, but on certain boats money can be saved by doing this job yourself.

If your boat is fitted with the flat perspex windows that are bolted through the cabin sides, using stainless steel bolts, replace-

A range of cleaning and maintenance products suitable for use on glass-fibre boats.

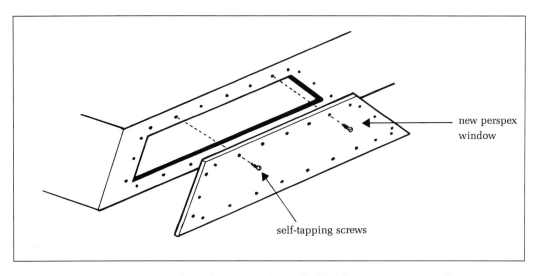

Fitting a replacement perspex window. The new window is bedded down on to mastic and aligned before tightening screws.

Using a putty filler to repair small cracks and holes in the deck of a boat. Once the filler has dried it can be sanded off before painting.

ment is simply a matter of unscrewing (or drilling out if riveted) the old bolts, taking care to save all the broken bits of perspex. A template can then be made in cardboard from the broken bits pieced together and a new window cut to shape from a fresh sheet of perspex. This can be bought from most DIY stores, either clear or with a smoked tint to it.

Once the new window has been cut to size and the edges chamfered down, it can be refitted to the boat using a good quantity of waterproof mastic as a seal all round. Use stainless steel taper bolts to refit and ensure that the new sheet is correctly seated before final tightening. On the inside of the cabin the heads of the bolts protruding can be cut off with a hacksaw and the nuts hidden by plastic caps (also available from DIY stores). A final polish to clean off any excess mastic is all that is required to finish the job.

The scratches and scuffs at the bow of this boat have been caused by a displaced fender – sometimes the fender itself will cause scuffing!

SUMMARY

- Your maintenance programme will proceed much more smoothly if you plan the various stages. Work back along the boat from bow to stern, noting down areas that will need attention. In this way, you will be able to assess the work involved and order your materials to match.

- When repairing holes or delamination, the gel coat will cure completely only if covered with a sheet of cellophane or Melinex, taped securely over the area.

- The deck fittings should be checked periodically for signs of looseness or damage. If necessary, remove the fitting, repair the damage and re-bed using a waterproof compound and bolts through to backing plates below decks.

4

OSMOSIS:
WHAT IT IS AND
HOW IT IS CURED

Mentioning the word 'osmosis' in the same breath as 'glass-fibre boat' usually brings on a cold sweat in owners of such craft. Osmosis, or 'boat pox' as it is commonly called, is a thing that was not supposed to happen. When glass-fibre boats were first introduced, back in the 1960s, glass fibre was hailed as the miracle material, the answer to every boat owner's dream: a craft that would not rot! It was not long, however, before this myth was exploded because glass fibre does, in fact, rot in its own particular way. The cause of this rot is called osmosis, although by common usage the cause has become synonymous with the result. Therefore, a boat which has osmosis is suffering from glass-fibre rot caused by osmosis.

What is it?

The dictionary description of osmosis is 'the attraction of a weak solution towards a strong solution'. In the case of a glass-fibre hull what happens is that water gradually penetrates the semi-permeable gel coat. There are a number of reasons for this happening, the main one being shoddy workmanship when the boat was initially built which causes impurities (holes, foreign bodies, trapped moisture, etc.) in the laminate and gel coat. Basically the poorer the standard of construction, the quicker the penetration of water will take place. The other main cause is the ingress of water from both outside and inside the boat. The purpose of this chapter, however, is not to look at the many reasons why osmosis starts but to look at the effect and cure.

As the moisture passes through the outer skin of the hull it forms a solution containing traces of styrene. Styrene is an essential component in the polyester resin used when the hull is first laid up and it is this which gives the distinct, chemically smell associated with new glass fibre.

This solution of water and styrene is stronger than the water on the outside of the hull and therefore osmosis (the attraction of the weaker solution to the stronger one) commences. As a general rule, fresh water is 'weaker' than salt water and craft that have been kept afloat on inland waterways tend to be more susceptible to osmosis than those which have spent all their lives immersed in sea

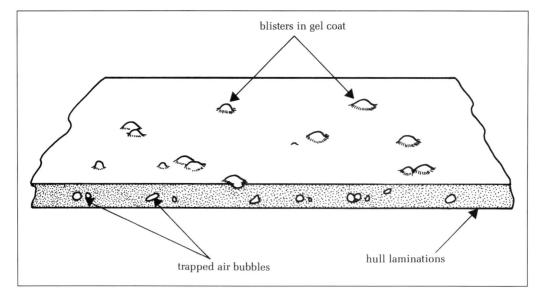

Osmotic blistering where air bubbles trapped in the laminations during the period the boat was built fill with moisture. Osmosis then causes pressure to build up forming blisters on the surface of the gel coat. When burst, these emit a vinegary smell as the moisture escapes.

A bad case of osmotic blistering on a glass-fibre hull. Note the many small blisters, some of which have burst and have let out fluid.

water. As the osmotic attraction of weak to strong continues, small voids will gradually be created behind the gel coat as more and more styrene dissolves into the water/styrene solution. As a result the solution becomes stronger and the osmotic attraction even greater, so that eventually pressure begins to build up within the void. This pressure will ultimately cause blistering of the gel coat which, as a result, becomes weaker, thereby permitting an even more rapid osmotic effect until, finally, the blister, which can be as small as a pin head, or the size of an egg in extreme cases, will burst leaving a crater-like cavity.

Results

The results of osmosis should be quite obvious when looking at a badly affected hull. However, in the early stages of its grip, or where a vessel has a thicker and hence stronger gel coat, it can be very difficult to diagnose. It will by now be equally obvious to the reader that osmosis need not be restricted to the part of the hull below the water-line which is in constant contact with the water. It can in fact occur in glass-fibre drinking-water tanks, the bilges, even badly designed scuppers which do not drain properly.

So, how do you know whether a boat is suffering from osmosis? There is only one

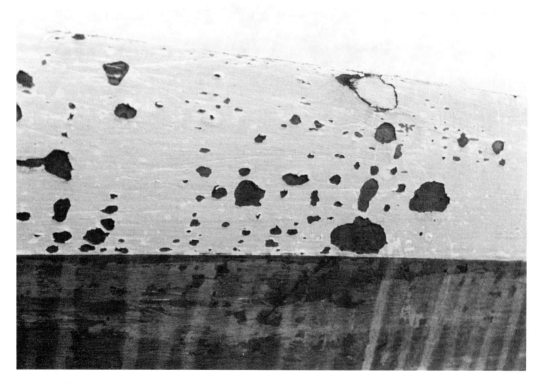

Extensive blistering on the hull of this boat just below the water-line has been cut and opened out before the drying-out process begins.

sure way to find out and that is to employ a marine surveyor who has both the expertise and equipment to trace and locate what could be very elusive signs, unless of course the problem is well advanced. There are a variety of moisture meters available on the market which can be used to detect the presence of moisture trapped in the laminate. When the meter's probe is placed against an area of blistering or wicking, the needle will register the moisture content at that point. If placed against a clean, moisture-free area of hull, the meter should not register. The meters vary considerably in their effectiveness and, of course, you not only have to know how to read them, but also how to translate this reading. Unfortunately, even the most inaccurate of these meters is not cheap and the more sophisticated ones, which would be the type used by a surveyor, could well cost a few hundred pounds, so you can see that investing in a professional survey which will cover all aspects of the craft, not just osmosis, is well worth the expense.

Using a moisture meter to detect the presence of water inside the glass-fibre laminate. The meter will register in areas with a moisture content, but there will be no reading in a dry, sound area.

It's got it, what do I do?

Your decision as to how to tackle the problem of osmosis will involve a great many options. If you are looking at a boat with a view to buying, you may decide that it is simply not worth the investment. Or, armed with the knowledge that some remedial work will need to be carried out, you may be able to haggle with the seller in order to reduce the price. Clearly this will depend on the extent of the problem and the total cost of remedying it. If you already own the boat you will probably have to face up to spending some money in order to repair the osmosis damage and prevent its recurrence. Remember, a boat with osmosis clearly will not sell as easily as one with a clean bill of health.

Treatments

What can be done about osmosis? First, prevention is obviously better than cure and if you have a new boat or one which has not yet started suffering from the dreaded glass-fibre rot, you may decide to have it treated with an epoxy system,

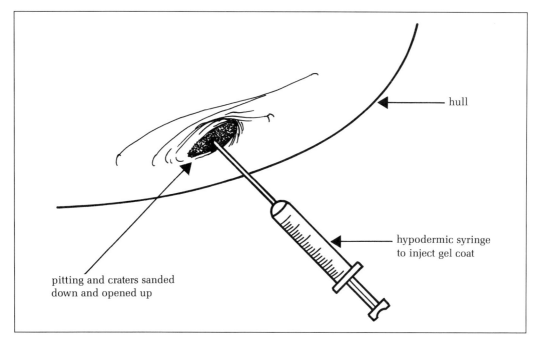

Small voids can be cut back and opened out. Gel coat can then be injected into the crater by using a hypodermic syringe.

something which can be readily tackled by the amateur yachtsman using a commercially available product, such as Gelshield or Osmaster. These treatments are described in greater detail later in this chapter. If you do not wish to treat the hull yourself, the boat should not be left in the water for more than two to three years at a time but should be slipped and regularly dried out. Unfortunately, even this action does not totally guarantee freedom from osmosis.

Assuming that your boat is suffering from osmosis there are two basic options open to you. One is to have your craft professionally treated by a specialist, of which there are several to choose from, situated at various locations around the coast, the other is to tackle the job

yourself, something which may not be quite as daunting as it at first sounds. Whichever way you choose, the first requirement is to get that hull dry. This can be achieved by simply storing the boat for a period out of the water or, for a quicker job, enclosing the hull in a plastic tent and using one or more dehumidifiers to extract all the moisture from the air surrounding the boat. The hull should be dried to approximately 5 per cent, although different treatments will be capable of tackling different levels of moisture content. Remember, it is impossible to dry out a hull completely; let's face it, whilst we are talking about GRP, just think what would happen to wood if you dried it out 100 per cent, you would be left with nothing but charcoal!

Professional Treatment

If you choose to have the work carried out by a boat-yard or treatment centre, there are basic stages involved after the hull has been dried out.

1. The entire area below the water-line will be sand blasted to remove the gel coat and expose all voids. Some yards may use one of the mechanical strippers now available on the market to remove the gel coat, although even this may involve sand blasting to reveal finally all voids.
2. The hull will then be filled and faired off to restore the underwater profile.
3. An epoxy treatment will be applied.

Doing the Job Yourself

1. The first stage, sand blasting, should be carried out by a professional, but do make sure it is somebody who knows what they are doing. A grit-blasting machine in the hands of the untrained, especially when used on a relatively soft material like glass fibre can be a lethal weapon and you

Antifouling paint being removed by grit blasting to prepare the surface of the gel coat for a protective epoxy coating. (Courtesy of International Paint.)

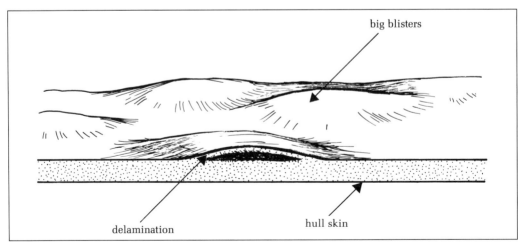

Bigger blistering may cause delamination where whole layers will start to peel back.

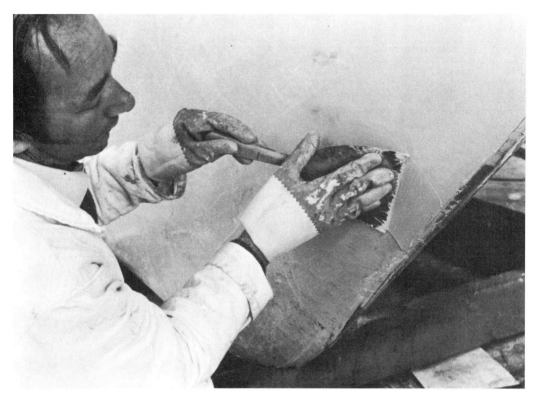

Using an epoxy filling compound to fill the surface of the hull after it has been grit blasted.
(Courtesy of International Paint.)

could end up with a boat that is nothing more than a mass of holes!

2. The second stage is the filling of the exposed holes, dents and voids; two conflicting views abound on the type of filling material which should be used. For some years epoxy fillers have been successfully used, but there have been several cases of this shelling off, a problem caused by the fact that epoxies have a mechanical adhesion to polyester, not a chemical one and absorb movement in a different way to the GRP hull. Therefore, if a thickish filling has been applied, the risk from this shelling effect is increased. If filling with an epoxy-based system, the sand-blasted surface would first be primed with a brush-on epoxy.

Using a polyester to fill will provide a material compatible with the hull and will allow you to make up your own filler using a polyester resin and 'microballoons'. Your chandler or local glass-fibre stockist will be able to supply these and help with mixing and application advice. Once the filler has been applied, usually by using a broad-bladed metal spatula, it should be faired off. Try and do as much as possible whilst the filler is in a partially cured state as this will be much easier and will reduce the need to do a great deal of sanding afterwards. This is particularly important if you chose to use an epoxy filler as they are by nature very hard when fully cured. 3. The final treatment should be carried out exactly as is about to be described for coating a hull which is either new or, as yet, has no osmosis. But remember, if you are treating a hull which has been filled, the filler **must** be allowed to cure thoroughly prior to the final treatment. At least one week should be allowed in the case of polyester but, if in any doubt, follow the manufacturer's advice.

Prevention is Better than Cure

It is possible to treat a hull which is not suffering from osmosis in order to prevent it from occurring. There are a number of epoxy-based products available for this purpose and the choice will depend very much upon the individual. The purpose of this chapter is not to examine the various merits, claimed or otherwise, of these products but to give examples of the materials available. Let us compare briefly those processes already mentioned. First, Gelshield, which is the system marketed

The first sealing coat of the Gelshield process is painted on to the surface of the hull after it has been grit blasted. (Courtesy of International Paint.)

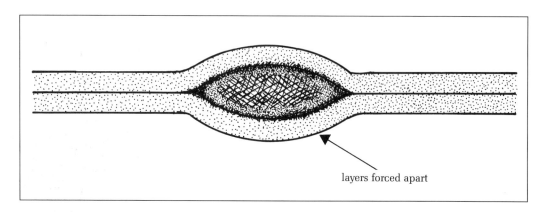

layers forced apart

Close-up of delamination.

by International Paint, is relatively thin and therefore a multi-coat system. At the other end of the scale, Osmaster, from the company of the same name, is an extremely high-build one-coat product which will save considerably on time, although it is fair to say that one coat of Osmaster will take longer to apply than a single coat of Gelshield. Osmaster is also safe for drinking water so can be used to line on-board water tanks.

In addition to having a dry hull, you will have to apply your epoxy coating within certain levels of humidity. Here you should closely follow the manufacturer's instructions, just as you should regarding sanding down the hull prior to application. As with any repair or painting work on a GRP boat, preparation is very important, even more so here, because there is no chemical bond between epoxies and polyesters, only a mechanical one. Epoxies have been proven to be very effective in preventing osmosis, due to their extremely low water absorbency levels. You should, however, be careful to

Close-up of moisture meter in use on a glass-fibre hull. Three scales are used here for different situations on GRP and timber boats. This type of meter is very portable and is small enough to be carried in a pocket.

choose a system which is solvent free as these are by far the best in terms of absorption. Epoxy pitches, for example, invariably contain some solvent.

SUMMARY

- Osmosis is caused by the attraction of a weak solution towards a stronger one. In the case of a glass-fibre boat, the water gradually permeates the semi-permeable gel coat (outer surface) into holes or voids left inside the glass-fibre laminate. The holes fill up with liquid and eventually expand to cause blisters on the outer surface of the boat.

- Your decision on how to tackle the problem of osmosis will depend on many factors. If you are looking at a boat with a view to buying, you may decide that if osmosis is present in a severe form, it may not be worth the investment.

- The prime job before tackling osmosis is to get the entire hull dry. Only then will the various treatments and cures be effective enough to stop the rot.

5
PRACTICAL PAINTING

It could once be said that painting glass fibre was for cosmetic purposes only, but with osmosis affecting some hulls and extensive repairs being made on others, together with the increasing number of people using epoxy-based coatings below the water-line, this is no longer the case. Most boat construction materials could benefit from a regular coat of paint once per season in order to protect them from the rigours of floating in salt or polluted water for months on end. Barnacles, algae and weed growth all take their toll on the hull and painting after a good clean down with a high-pressure hose and scrubber is an excellent way of restoring a boat to her former glory.

Whatever material your craft is built of you will only really achieve a first-class finish if your preparation of the surface to be painted is strict and thorough. It is the initial preparation that will make or break the final result, so time spent wisely will pay dividends in the end. It does not take an expert to slap on a coat of paint, but a little extra effort in preparing the ground will be handsomely repaid. If new paint is simply splodged on, covering up all the old blemishes, cuts and cracks, instead of an improved appearance, the result will be only to highlight the problems and cause new paint to flake off with the old, which is a total waste of both time and money. Apart from the protection that a good-quality paint job affords the boat, it is also

New glass-fibre boats will not normally require painting during their first few years, but on older, second-hand craft or boats that have been neglected, a coat of paint will eventually be required to keep them looking good and to protect them from the rigours of the weather.

the criteria by which the boat owner and the craft are judged. There is nothing quite like cruising along in a boat that has been well maintained, attracting admiring glances as you go!

A boat will soon become tatty and unsightly if left uncared for. Just look at the state of the varnish work on the bulkhead of this cruiser that has been left with its canopy blown off by the wind over the winter months.

Tools

The tools required for painting are, like the ones used in glass-fibre work, simple and uncomplicated. A cheapish orbital sander with various grades of wet-and-dry paper is ideal for sanding down large areas of the hull or superstructure, while a simple hand-sanding block will be useful for smaller areas. Paintbrushes should be chosen with care. Buy the best you can afford, it is cheaper in the long run as the brush will last for years and a good one will not shed hairs over the work, which is something that drives me mad! Several

A hand-sanding block is ideal for rubbing down small areas, and you will be able to control the pressure applied more easily than with a power-driven sander.

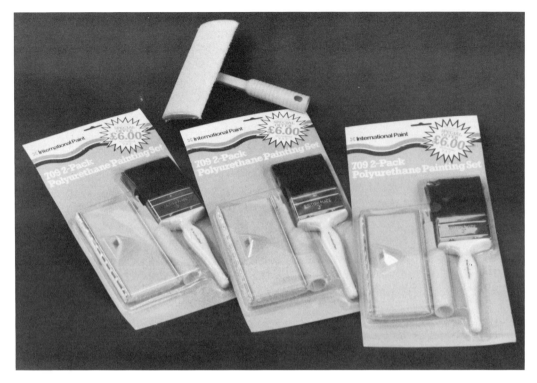

Good-quality paintbrushes are essential if a smooth, professional finish is to be achieved. These brushes and paint pads from International Paint have been specially developed for use with their two-pack polyurethane paint system, 709.

sizes ranging from 15mm (½in) up to about 75mm (3in) should suffice, along with a big tin of brush cleaner. Scrapers and a good, flexible-bladed knife for filling and a selection of sanding papers will also be needed. Use grades from 80 to 100 grit paper on the orbital sander for coarse rubbing down and 320 grit paper for hand sanding between coats. A medium grade should be used for general sanding.

Brush Care

Brushes are expensive items and you should always buy the very best you can afford if you want to prevent hairs from pulling out and marring the finished coat. Brush care is easy but so often neglected. In our local marina I frequently find perfectly serviceable and often expensive brushes discarded in the marina rubbish bins, caked hard with old paint because their owners could not be bothered to clean them properly. If the paint is of the conventional type then I have no qualms about rescuing these brushes from the bin, soaking them in brush cleaner for a few days, after which they are fully serviceable again. It is not generally realized that a new brush will give a rougher finish than an old one which has been in use for some time and, like a cheap brush, will shed hairs on the painted surface when first used. A set of good brushes will benefit any type of painting; washing immediately after use will ensure a long life, even with two-pack epoxy paints.

Paint Systems

The paint systems used for glass fibre can roughly be divided into four types: the more traditional yacht enamels, the one-pack polyurethanes, two-pack epoxy coatings and two-pack polyurethanes. The traditional types are usually cheaper and are easier to apply, but will require frequent recoating whereas the newer two-pack systems give very hard-wearing, durable finishes which, when correctly applied, give an outstanding high-gloss finish. This gloss is one of the main reasons for sound preparatory work before painting commences as it tends to show up every blip and blemish in the coated surface. Once you have decided upon the paint system, you can start the preparation work.

Preparation

The first thing to do is to wash down the entire hull and topsides with a suitable glass-fibre degreasing agent. International Yacht Paints make a good degreaser that is applied and then left for several minutes to allow it to start emulsifying any grease or polish that may be left on the surface. This is particularly important because unless the hull is scrupulously clean, any primer or top coat applied to it will simply not adhere and will eventually flake off. After applying the degreaser, thoroughly wash

the hull with clean, warm water. No detergent should be used as this too can leave deposits that might adversely affect the finished paint coat. Look closely at the hull when wet. Does the water break up into small droplets? If it does, this indicates that some grease is still present and further degreasing will be required. If the boat has been regularly coated with a high-quality wax, a solvent cleaner may have to be used to break this up.

Once the hull is completely clean, you can start to fill all the cracks and blemishes using a selection of fillers and dressing cements compatible with your chosen paint system. The fillers are generally used to fill the larger cracks and dents, while the dressing cements are used for skim-filling the more minor pits and surface holes. It is essential to use the correct type of filler and cement to give good adhesion when the final top coats are applied. Check that every blemish has been filled, no matter how small. (I once read of a magnifying glass being used to check for pin holes and this seems like good advice.) It cannot be emphasized how important it is to eradicate imperfections. Any remaining ones will show up as if by magic as soon as the gloss coat is applied!

Any serious hull damage that involves punctures through the laminate of the hull should be repaired from the inside, cutting back the damaged rough edges and building up at least five layers of matting, stippled down well with resin. The outside can then be built up using crumbled up bits of chopped strand mat and catalyzed resin pushed into the hole to within 3mm (⅛in) from the outside surface. Once this has thoroughly cured, a layer of gel coat can be trowelled in, covered in cellophane which is taped

67

down, and then smoothed out using a squeegee. The reason for using the cellophane is to ensure that the gel coat cures completely and does not remain tacky. Examine the repair for shrinkage and refill if necessary. Once the filling stage has been completed, the individual repairs and then the whole hull should be rubbed down using a 280-grade wet-and-dry abrasive paper, removing the dust and debris as you go. Refer to Chapter 3 for further details of general repairs to glass fibre.

Rubbing down is probably one of the most boring jobs in boat maintenance but it is also the most important part of the preparation process. There are one or two tips that if followed during sanding will help you to achieve a first-rate coat. The choice of sander can have a marked effect on the quality of finish. A belt-driven sander is easy to control but you can get carried away, putting on more and more pressure until a groove builds up in the surface. Disc sanders are difficult to control and can cause unsightly round gouges which can be more difficult to remove than the blemish or repair you were rubbing down. The best sander is the orbital one. Designed for light work, it is easy to control the applied pressure and will produce an even-sanded effect. For large areas the power sander is ideal as it takes much of the arm ache out of rubbing

An electric drill fitted with a small sanding pad is ideal for rubbing down paintwork in preparation for filling, prior to a fresh coat.

Rotary sanding discs of different grades can be used with a power drill for sanding larger areas.

down, but for smaller sanding jobs such as smoothing out repairs to cracks and holes, a hand-sanding block would be more effective. These are formed from a block of hard cork (do not use timber which could, if used irregularly, cause deep scratching in a glass-fibre surface), with the sanding paper wrapped around it. Used correctly, more pressure can be put behind the paper giving a more even effect.

When starting to rub down, use a coarse grade of paper first to remove most of the rough material and old paint to a level which will be made up by the new coat. It is important to remove as many coats of old paint as you will be replacing with new, otherwise, over the years, too thick a coating will build up, eventually causing a breakdown in the surface with splitting and flaking the result.

Small scrapers of various shapes and sizes are useful for removing flaking paint.

Area to be painted		Formula
Bottoms		Full-bodied craft such as steam or motor yachts, shallow draft yachts and straight long keeled yachts. L.W.L × (B + D) = Area in square metres
		Medium draft sailing cruisers with rounded bows. 0.75 × L.W.L × (B + D) = Area in square metres
		Deep-keeled racing craft, cut away forward with short keels. 0.50 × L.W.L × (B + D) = Area in square metres
Topsides		(L.O.A + B) × 2 times Average Free Board = Area in square metres
Decks		(L.O.A + B × 0.75) = Area in square metres Note: The area taken up by a coach roof, cockpit etc. will have to be subtracted in many cases.

The above formulae can be used to calculate the likely paint requirements for any given boat. They are based on a study done by International Paint on the most accurate practical coverage and spreading rate per litre, per coat. L.O.A. = length overall, L.W.L. = Length of water-line, B = Beam, D = Draft, Freeboard = Water-line to deck level. (Courtesy of International Yacht Paints.)

Once the hull has been thoroughly degreased, holes and blemishes filled, and the whole area rubbed down, it is now time to start the painting process. For this description we will use a two-pack polyurethane paint system, such as International Paint's Perfection 709. It is a very popular type and, if applied properly under the right conditions, gives an excellent high-gloss finish. The paint itself is a polyester-based substance and as such is very suitable for application to glass-fibre surfaces.

Primer

The first coat is usually the priming coat and is used to give a key to the surface to allow the other paint coats to adhere. Special glass-fibre primers are available which react chemically with the polyester gel coat giving excellent bonding and maximum adhesion for the other paint coats. Usually one coat is sufficient, the primer can be thinned as required and application is either by brush, roller or spray. Once dry, the next stage is to use an undercoat, especially if the colour of the hull or topsides is to be changed. Perfection 709 undercoat should be used for the two-pack system, leaving at least 16 hours between coats. International recommend that the undercoat should be rubbed down using a 280-320 grade of wet-and-dry paper if the undercoat has been left for more than 36 hours before recoating. It is usual to use two coats of undercoat with filling, as necessary, using dressing cement between coats, followed by a light rub down and finishing off with two top coats, applied with close reference to the manufacturer's instructions.

Working Conditions

If you are intending to spend the money on applying a top-quality, two-pack epoxy paint system it will be worth taking the time to study the manufacturer's recommendations on working conditions, such as temperature, overcoating times and especially mixing ratios. Although you will probably never quite achieve the exact ideal conditions for all aspects, the closer you come to them the better will be the finished job. If possible, wait for a spell of warm, dry weather and complete your paint job inside. Many boats are painted 'on the hard', i.e. chocked up on supports in the marina park or boat-yard so a temporary cover, rigged perhaps over the boom on one side of the boat, will afford some protection when painting.

A poor flow of fresh air around the boat will impede the drying process, increasing the time taken for the paint to dry and a humid atmosphere may even result in epoxy systems undercuring as the curing agent reacts to the moisture in the air. However, in making sure that you have adequate ventilation, do not use electric fans which will stir up unwanted dust and impair the finished paintwork.

If you find you are having problems with osmosis, the paint system chosen, or just want to apply an epoxy scheme to the bottom of your craft, then a discussion with the paint manufacturer will be a great help; try to speak directly with the manufacturer's technical department, if possible.

Painting

Decks

When using high-performance paint systems the manufacturer will usually recommend a two-pack polyurethane for the decks, with silver sand sprinkled into the last coat, followed by a light finishing coat over the sanded surface. I prefer to use the conventional non-slip paint, masked off into areas and applied over the final coat of two-pack polyurethane which should be lightly sanded to give a good key.

Bilges

Another important area requiring an effective paint coat is the bilges, especially in the engine compartment. This should be carried out by the boat builder during construction to prevent the ingress of water into the laminate during the boat's life, but unfortunately many boats are left unpainted in this area. On a new boat it will not be a big job to apply a coat of glass-fibre primer followed by two coats of bilge paint, however, on a older boat where the bilges have never been painted, they are sure to be damp and dirty, necessitating

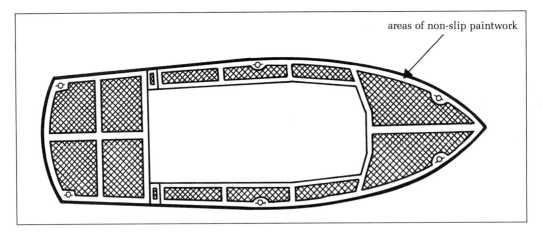

areas of non-slip paintwork

The deck of a boat can be masked off into zones before painting with non-slip deck paint.

a thorough cleaning. This should be followed by a prolonged period with the floorboards raised, enabling the whole area to dry out properly.

If the bilges are not completely dry when the initial coat of primer is applied, it will not adhere properly, making the job useless. It can sometimes take several months for the bilges to dry out thoroughly, but if the job is tackled in the winter when the boat is laid up ashore it will be a worthwhile step in prolonging its life.

Water-line

One painting job which seems to strike fear into the hearts of most DIY boat owners is the repainting or retouching of the boot top and water-line. These are the separation zones that break up the antifouling paint on the hull bottom, the area of the hull from antifouling to gunwhale level and the trim line, normally just below the gunwhale. Get the finish lines of these painted zones off skew and the overall look of the boat in the water will be marred.

However old the boat, unless the state of the hull is in a very poor condition or all the top coat of paint has been taken off, there should still be some indication of the water-line and boot top which should make the job of repainting simple. If the boat is regularly used at sea and is immersed for most or all of a season, a good quality antifouling paint should be used when painting in the boot top. Hull and water-line paint can be chosen from the wide variety on the market, but twin-pack polyurethane is probably the best as it is extremely hard-wearing and holds its colour well.

The first step in your painting sequence is to paint the topsides down to below the level of the boot top. When this has dried and/or cured, the boot top line should be masked off using a good quality masking tape (cheap tapes are useless and produce nicks in the paint when removed) at least 25mm (1in) in width.

The next step is to paint up from below the water-line on to, but not across the masking tape. Remove the tape before the paint is quite dry; if you don't you will

Using a good-quality masking tape to mask off the boot top line prior to painting.

find that the hardened coat of paint overlapping the tape will chip off, causing a jagged and unsightly line. Tacky paint tears in a smooth, clean action leaving a crisp, knife-edged line. Some paint systems, such as certain brands of two-pack epoxy, will seep through the masking tape, causing the same sort of untidy edge when the tape is peeled back. For a really clean line do not use cheap or ordinary masking tape, use a special type, such as Fineline 218 which is marketed by the 3M Group. When the boot top is fully dry, mask off the water-line position and apply your antifouling up to the masking tape, which is then removed in the same sequence as above.

This is not as difficult as it may at first seem. If you have the original plans of the boat, measurements can be taken down at several points (bow, stern, amidships) from the side elevation. If no plans are available, try to find a boat of the same class and size, or if all else fails, sight the water-line by eye.

Once you have marked your stem and stern points, timber supports can be rigged either by forming an 'A' frame or by driving a post into the ground at the correct spot. A string line, weighted at each end, can then be run from each post. To mark the line on the boat, the string is simply moved against the hull and a small pencil mark made at the point where the line touches. The sequence is repeated for the other side of the boat.

The boot top is slightly different as it curves. Two battens should be set inclined to the levelled ones at each end. The boot top should be about 75–90mm (3.0–3.5in) above the water line at the bow and 40–50mm (1.6–2.0in) above it at the amidships point. At the stern it will be approximately 60–70mm (2.4–2.8in) above. The inclined battens can be adjusted until the string meets the boot top marks at each end. Once this is done the rest of the line should lie parallel and above the water-line for most of the length of the craft. To paint it in, simply mark in the line with a pencil and mask off as before checking that the finished line is true before applying the paint.

Another method of applying a non-slip surface to the deck of a boat is to use self-adhesive strips which can be purchased in a variety of widths, lengths and colours to match most boats. They are easy to apply and are ideal for smaller craft or for laying non-slip on narrow or awkward areas.

SUMMARY

- Preparation is the key word before starting any paint job on the boat. Some time spent preparing the surface for painting will pay dividends in a superb, glossy finish of which you will be proud. No preparation will result in a lack-lustre finish that will soon revert to being in need of repainting.

- If you are intending to spend money on applying a top-quality, two-pack epoxy paint system, it will be worth taking the time to study the manufacturer's recommendations on working conditions.

- Use only the best masking tape you can afford in order to avoid the annoying 'nicking' that can occur as paint wicks under a cheap tape to impinge on the next colour layer. A good quality tape such as Fineline 218 from 3M is a good one to use.

6

SYSTEMS MAINTENANCE

Do-it-yourself maintenance is one of the more pleasurable aspects of owning a boat and for most boat owners it is part of the overall enjoyment they get from their hobby. It is not only an excellent way of gaining knowledge in terms of finding out how each part of the boat works, being able to repair it in an emergency, and knowing that it will perform perfectly under power or sail, but also in the money saved on potentially expensive boat-yard bills. Many of the general maintenance and service tasks aboard a boat can be undertaken by the keen amateur with a modicum of skills and a good toolkit. This chapter looks at the various aspects of boat maintenance involving the separate systems on a boat; steering and control gear, toilets, plumbing, gas systems, ropes and rigging.

Every boat requires regular maintenance if it is to perform well at sea. Apart from the pride that owners will get from their craft, well-maintained boats will also be safe boats in the respect that fewer equipment failures will be likely. A boat owner who never even thinks of doing any remedial repairs or servicing is sure to come unstuck, usually in the most inconvenient and dangerous place. The likelihood of engine or electrical system failure or rigging faults occurring will be greatly increased on a boat that receives little or no maintenance.

Making a Plan

Before starting any maintenance it will be best to sit down in the cabin with a pad and pencil and plan out the areas you will need to cover. This will include the engines, stern gear (propeller shaft, couplings, etc.), steering and control system, the electrical system, toilet and plumbing system, gas installation and, on a sailing yacht, the running and standing rigging. As you make your list, walk around the boat examining the various systems and noting down items which require attention. By doing this you will be able to order spare parts before you start your maintenance programme. Once you have made your list, ordered your spares and got together a toolkit, you can make a start. Because they are quite large subjects, inboard and outboard engines are covered in Chapter 7.

Gas Systems

Most types of boat, whatever their size, if fitted with cooking or heating equipment

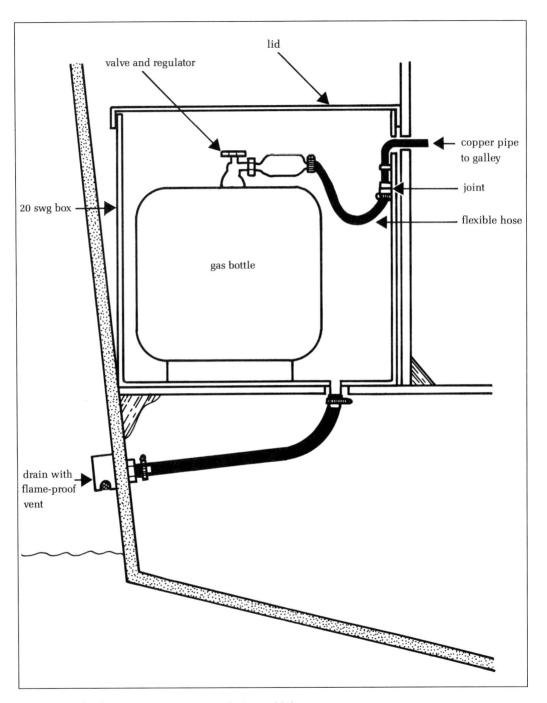

A typical gas-bottle compartment, note ventilation and lid.

are probably also fitted with a bottled gas supply. The type used is liquid petroleum gas (LPG) and is a highly volatile substance contained under liquid pressure in a metal cylinder. It is supplied in two types, butane and propane. Because of its use in the relatively confined space of a boat, the gas system can be dangerous if neglected or treated with disrespect. It is the duty of boat owners to ensure the safety of their gas installations and a regular inspection should be carried out at least twice every season, and definitely at the end of the year.

For boat owners wanting to know about the ins and outs of actually installing an LPG system, leaflets are available from Calor Gas, the British Standards Institute or from the Coastguard. The gas bottle itself should be fitted into a fully ventilated compartment, preferably outside the main cabins of the boat. On most modern cruisers the gas supply can be found mounted in special lockers on the stern deck. These are self-draining for both water and gas which, being heavier than air, sinks to the lowest point available, which in the case of a boat is the bilges! If you are fitting a new locker make sure that it is mounted where it cannot receive the direct rays of the sun, but will not immediately freeze over in the winter if you cruise all year. Butane, especially, will freeze up and become useless at just below freezing point, particularly if the bottle is left outside overnight. For year-round boaters, propane gas would be the better choice.

Leaks

If you suspect that there has been a leakage of gas, it is no use trying to pump it overboard with the bilge pump. It will not

work and, as the pump is electrically operated could well generate sparks, which is not recommended! The first thing to do is to switch off all the boat's electrical systems, including lights. Do not, however, attempt to disconnect the main storage battery in case you inadvertently cause a spark. Turn off the gas at the cylinder and open up the hatches or remove floorboards to gain access to the bilge area. This sounds silly but, using a plastic bucket, bail out the gas. There really is no better way of removing a large quantity of gas from the bottom of a boat.

Detectors and 'Sniffers'

There are several good gas detectors available which have 'sniffers' that will detect a gas leak at very low levels. They range in size, complexity and price but would be well worth the trouble of fitting. When a leak is detected a loud alarm, or

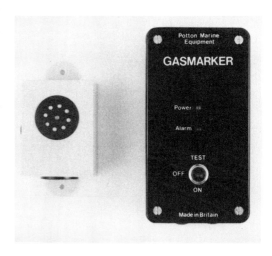

Fitting a gas detector gives peace of mind. There are several types on the market usually comprising a 'sniffer' unit positioned in a suitable place near the bilge and an alarm.

light, or both, goes off to warn of the problem. Once you have removed most of the gas from the boat, open up all windows and ventilators to allow a good draught of fresh air through the craft.

Gas pipework should be of the seamless copper type and should be regularly inspected for signs of stress or fatigue, especially at joints and appliances. Make sure that pipes are clipped up at regular intervals (at least every 15cm (6in)) and that all joints are visible and accessible. Check the gas-tightness of a joint by swabbing the area with a solution of soapy water applied with a paintbrush. You will soon see if even a small leak is present. There is also a safe gas-leak detection solution contained in a convenient aerosol spray can that can be bought for this purpose. Sometimes a joint will simply need retightening, but replacement could be the result of a badly leaking one. It goes without saying, but **never** search for a gas leak with a naked flame!

Safety First

When you leave the boat, always switch off the gas supply at the main cylinder which will take the pressure off the pipework and will reduce the possibility that a leaky joint or valve might start a build-up of gas in the boat when it is unattended.

When fitting a new system or over-hauling an existing one, make sure that each appliance or gas outlet is fitted with its own isolating tap so that that particular section can be closed off. Keep the taps themselves freely movable so that they may be turned off in an emergency.

A further safety angle involves re-membering that gas heaters and other appliances burn up oxygen from the cabin

and therefore adequate ventilation must be provided. Apart from the obvious open window, fixed ventilators should be mounted near cookers and behind fridges and as near as possible to heaters. Some heaters that are mounted near the floor, of the catalytic type, may be able to be supplied with air from the bilge, the heat drawing up the fresh air. Whichever method you employ, ensure an adequate, free-moving supply of fresh air when using all LPG appliances.

Toilet Systems

The toilet should be serviced occasionally to keep it working efficiently. There is nothing quite so bad as a broken toilet, especially on a long sea passage! Some boats fitted with simple chemical toilets require only regular emptying and recharging with the correct solution of chemical fluid and water for flushing. Holding tank toilets have a special tank, usually installed under the toilet itself, which is used to store the waste until it can be pumped out at the marina or waterside pump-out station. A machine sucks out the waste, replacing it with fresh water and chemical solution. Some of these toilets can be discharged overboard at sea, although in these environmentally aware times it is not recommended.

Maintenance for the sea-type toilet is confined to making sure that the sea-cock inlet and outlets are working correctly and that their gate valves open and close freely. Dismantle and lubricate as re-quired, replacing any worn parts. If a smell starts to pervade your toilet compartment, this could be due to the gland packing on the main pump shaft becoming worn or that the valves have

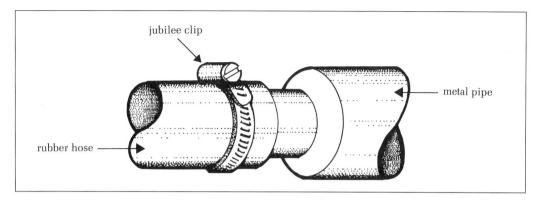

The correct method of securing a rubber hose to a metal pipe is to use a jubilee-type clip. Pipe clips on toilet and plumbing systems should be regularly checked and tightened, replacing when worn or rusting.

become stuck. Close the sea cocks, then dismantle the pipes to clear any blockage which might have become wedged. Check all inlet and outlet pipes regularly for signs of leakage, tightening hose clips as required. The toilet itself needs little maintenance, apart from regular cleaning of the bowl and surrounding attachments.

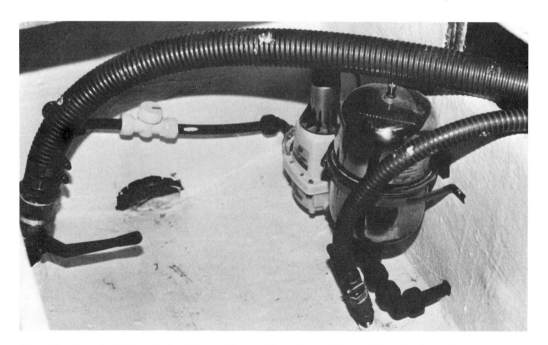

Sea-cock valves should be checked for smooth operation, dismantling and cleaning the valve seats, if required. At the same time check the security of all hose clips and the state of the pipework.

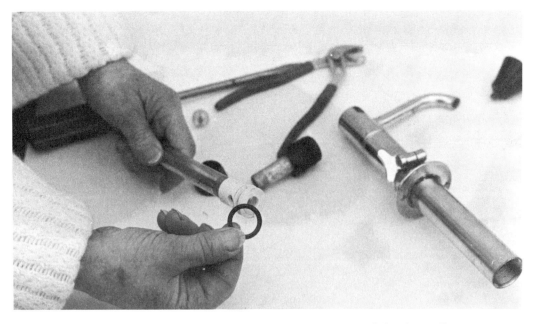

One of the most common parts of a hand-operated domestic water pump to fail is the small rubber 'O' ring at the base of the plunger, causing leaks and inefficient operation. It is a simple matter to dismantle the pump and replace the ring.

Plumbing

Many boat owners who have fallen foul of mysterious illnesses often blamed on food poisoning or sea-sickness could really have been suffering from a contaminated water supply. Needless to say, the boat water tanks should always be filled from a drinking water supply. This is particularly important when going foreign.

It is always a good idea to keep the water flowing through your system at regular intervals. This will prevent any build-up of bacteria in the pipes. Any water, however fresh when piped in, will eventually become contaminated if it is stored in the closed system of a boat. This will show up in bad smells and tastes and the complete system will eventually need flushing out with a cleansing chemical.

Bad smells and brackish-tasting water can usually be overcome and one of the simplest ways is chlorination of the water, using special tablets. The tablets are particularly useful on long trips where a large amount of water has to be stored, and in foreign waters where the supply of drinking water may be dubious.

You can also fit special purifiers which filter the water as it is being drawn off. These are usually fitted into the main supply line from the pump simply by splicing them into the pipework and clipping them in place. Every two years, flush the entire system through with a mild bleach, followed by plenty of fresh water and try to look inside the ends of pipes to check for the growth of algae. In the spring, when the system is to be refilled, connect the hoses back on to the main water pump and tighten any drain screws you left open. Fill the water system and run the taps for about ten minutes to help remove any dirt. Make sure that there are no leaks from hoses and that couplings in plastic pipes are tight and secure.

Steering System

Check the operation and security of the steering and control gear. Control cables should be examined for damage where they pass through tight bulkheads and around severe corners, and the open ends greased at the engine where brass flanges and cotter pins should also be inspected. This is the point at which most control cables fail, by snapping from the engine.

Control boxes can be dismantled and regreased with each operating mode

The ends of gear and throttle control cables are the parts most susceptible to wear and failure. Examine them for signs of splits in the outer jacket and check the linkage where the cables are joined to the engine.

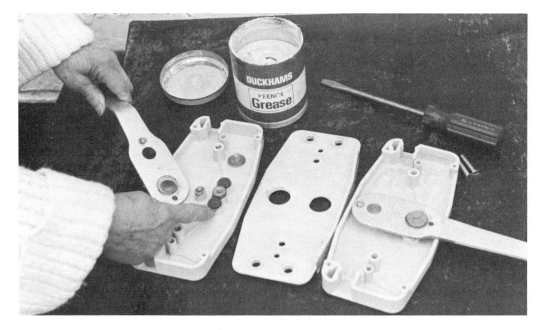

Throttle and gearshift control boxes can be dismantled and the bushes and pivots given a light coating of waterproof grease.

checked for smoothness of movement. On rack and cable steering, remove the covers to inspect the cogs which should be greased with an appropriate lubricant. Check for wear in the bearings and make sure that the central nut on the steering wheel is tight and secure. At the rudder end, the pintles and gudgeons should be inspected for excessive wear and replaced as required. Check the rudder post bearings for leakage and reduce any slackness or movement between the tiller and rudder stock. If the boat has been slipped or the water sufficiently clear enough to see, test the operation of each trim tab, removing any growth that may have attached itself on the rams and tab plates.

Smaller craft may have been fitted with cable and pulley steering, so check the free movement of the cables around the pulleys and that the small clamps that hold the cable ends in position as they

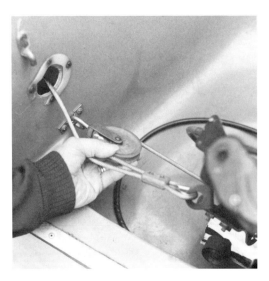

Check the condition of cables and pulleys on cable steering systems, tightening cable clamps and putting a drop of oil on the centres of the pulleys.

pass around the spring catchboys are tight. A drop of light oil or spray of WD40 on the pulley shafts will aid movement, and don't forget to examine the plastic coating on the cable for hardening.

Rigging Systems

The rigging on the topsides of a sailing yacht can make the on-deck maintenance much more arduous and complicated than that of a power boat. The main thing is to ensure that all screws are tight and that any that have come loose are either tightened or replaced. This goes for cleats, fairleads and bollards as well as genoa tracks, mainsheet travellers, cam cleats and grab rails. Any moving parts on tracks, cam cleats and winches should be lubricated, with individual winches dismantled for servicing as required. Suspect a winch that has become particularly free when turned as it might mean that an internal part has come loose or broken free, which could jam the winch at an inopportune moment.

Shackles and snatch blocks should have damaged or missing pins replaced and oiled as required. Check wire hawsers for 'fish-hooks' which are individual strands of wire that have broken and turned back. They can be a menace to sails and give nasty cuts to bare hands. Cut them off with wire shears and tape over the area using self-amalgamating tape. If the cable has many such hooks, it might need replacing.

Sea rails and their associated stanchions and wires should be checked for security and bottle screws tightened to retension the wires as required. Check the stanchion bases for loose screws or signs of stress which could indicate that a stanchion is going to pull out. Turnbuckles and other

Rigging should be examined for signs of wear. Shroud plates and load-bearing items should be checked for security of fixing, tracks and running rigging should be lubricated as required.

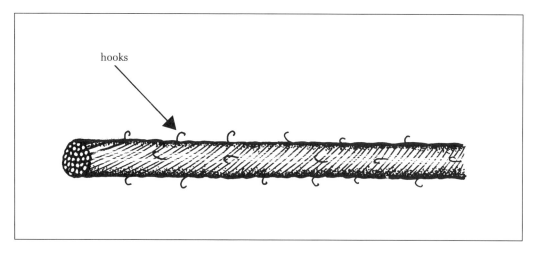

hooks

Fish hooks in wire rope can be dangerous to the unprotected hand. Small numbers of hooks can be cut off using snips, but more serious fraying may mean that the whole hawser will require replacement.

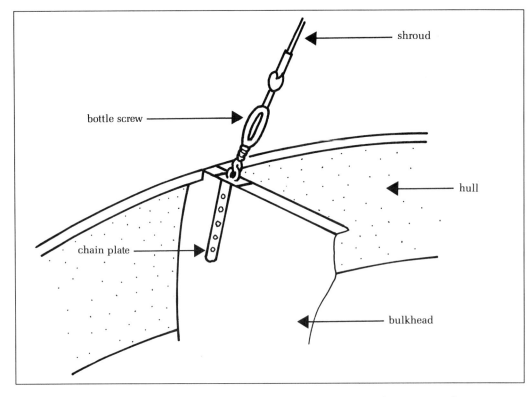

The chain plate at the point where the shroud is fixed to the boat is an area of great stress. Plates should be checked for security, tightening loose bolts where necessary.

sharp fittings should be protected by wrapping around anti-chafing tape. This stops unnecessary tears to sails or clothing which might otherwise be caught.

The shrouds that support the mast are secured to the boat by special plates, called chain plates, attached to bulkheads or gussets below deck. Check that the bolts are tight and that the straps are still straight and securely fitted. Remember great strain is placed on this type of fitting! All parts of the standing rigging (spars, mast, shrouds, stays, spreaders, etc.) should be regularly examined for wear or failure. Work down from the masthead, if necessary rigging a bos'n's chair to reach

The shrouds that support the mast are secured by plates which are usually subjected to great strain. They should be regularly inspected for stress cracks and looseness.

the top of the mast. Most boats use stainless steel for their standing rigging which usually withstands wear and tear, but some use older-style galvanized fittings which can be more susceptible to corrosion. These should receive more regular checks.

Remove rust deposits with a wire brush or light sanding, then grease or spray with WD40 as required. Mast and boom tracks should be regularly lubricated. One simple method is to apply the lubricating oil to the first slide and hoist the sail, which allows the other slides to take the oil up the track as they go. Check the gooseneck where the boom is attached to the mast, once again lubricating as necessary.

Ropes

Most good-quality ropes are expensive to buy and a little thought and attention to them occasionally will prolong their life and ensure that failure during use is minimized.

Remove dirt, grit and other foreign bodies that may have become embedded in the rope. These may well cause unseen internal wear. Wash your ropes thoroughly with clean, fresh water and allow them to dry outside. Never use any kind of detergents on ropes containing natural fibres.

Rope deteriorates rapidly if subjected to rough surfaces. Check your fairleads, winches and bollards for sharp projections, and examine your ropes regularly. If your lines display a slightly fluffy appearance this may be due to normal wear and should not have any drastic effects on the strength of the rope. All ropes should be stowed away from heat, boilers, pipes and from long periods in the sun. Chemicals are a danger, especially to man-made fibre ropes, so keep all solutions away from rope lockers. Try to prevent the rope from becoming kinked or distorted. If a rope develops a kink, it is a sure indication that it has been badly mishandled. Care should be taken to try to remove the trouble. Kinking of rope is usually caused by excessive rotating against the weave and lay.

Dealing with Frayed Ropes

Frayed and tattered ropes not only lower the general appearance of the craft to which they are tied, but could also eventually lead to the rope breaking. At the very least this could cause embarrassment for the owner in front of fellow boat owners, but at worst the craft could be lost, having broken its moorings.

In almost every case the prime cause of a rope's downfall is a fraying loose end. The sailor's art of whipping includes several methods by which a rope's ends may be bound to prevent fraying. It may not be an art that is totally dying, as it is still no doubt widely used by older sailors and enthusiasts, but it has become somewhat neglected due in no short measure to the advent of synthetic rope whose ends can simply be heat sealed. Indeed, in many chandleries synthetic rope is cut to length with a heated blade which seals both ends and cuts it at the same time.

This is as far as many owners go, but with frequent use, the sealed ends start to crack and if not tended to will eventually fray out. A small back-up whipping applied to the rope will prevent this happening. Whipping can also be used to mark the centre of a line or, when applied to the spoke of a steering wheel, can tell you when the rudder is ahead.

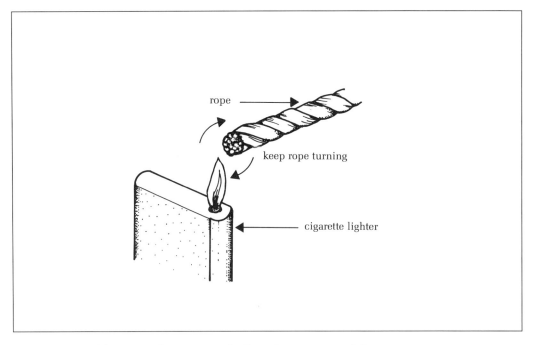

rope

keep rope turning

cigarette lighter

Sealing the end of the man-made rope using the flame from a cigarette lighter.

For small-diameter ropes the whipping should be approximately as long as the diameter of the rope itself, and on ropes with a diameter over 12mm (½in) the whipping should be about three-quarters of this measurement.

The whipping should finish about 8mm (⅓in) from the end of the rope, and any finishing knots or loose ends of twine should be tucked in. Before the whipping is applied, use heat sealing to prevent the strands of synthetic rope from fraying while you work. Heat up the end with a gas flame or cigarette lighter (a match only blackens the nylon) and when soft, roll the end of the rope or each individual lay between your moistened fingers to keep the size of the seal as close to the rope's original diameter as possible. Keep the rope turning to avoid overheating and possible melting.

Common Whipping

There are several ways to make a plain or common whipping, but all achieve much the same result. The end of the whipping twine is laid along the length of the rope and several tight turns are made over it, the twine is then doubled back on itself and the rest of the turns completed over it. Pass the working end of the twine through this bight (which is pulled tight) and draw it down under the final turns. Both the projecting ends may then be cut off, and tucked neatly into the weave. A tighter and perhaps stronger method is to make the initial turns over the start of the twine which can then be cut off. The final three or four turns are loosely made so that the working end may be passed under them, pulled tight and then cut and tied.

Making an Eye Splice

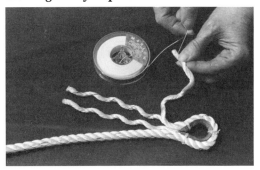

(a) Place a metal thimble into the lay of the rope and apply three seizings, using whipping twine to hold it in position. Allow about 15cm (6in) of free end. Unlay the rope back to the throat of the thimble and apply a small whipping to each end.

(b) Insert a Swedish fid into the lay of the rope and, taking the centre strand, pass its tail through the fid.

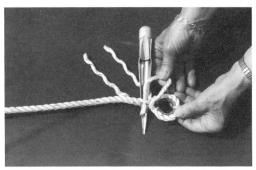

(c) Pull the strand tight, insert the fid and pass the right-hand strand of the remaining two through it, tightening in the same way.

(d) Do the same with the remaining strand, then pull all three tight, snuggling them down into the lay of the rope.

(e) Each free end should now be tucked over the strand to its left in turn, forming a neat pattern until each free end has been fully tucked in.

(f) Tuck the remaining stubs into the weave of the rope and remove the whipping twine from the thimble, which should now be held tight and secure in the finished splice.

Whipping

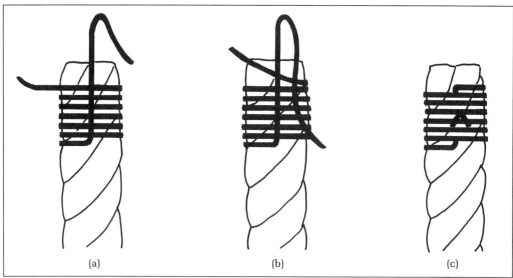

(a)   (b)   (c)

(a) The end of the whipping twine is laid along the length of the rope and several tight turns are made over it. (b) The twine is then doubled back on itself and the rest of the turns made over it. Pass the end of the rope through the loop formed. (c) The end is then pulled tight and drawn down under the final turns before being cut off and tucked in.

Follow these simple measures and your ropes should last you a lifetime or at least for the duration of time that you own the boat. It is surprising the number of boat owners who become so attached to their favourite rope that they usually travel with them from boat to boat leaving a new set of lines aboard for each new owner which is a sure sign of the affection of mariners for their lifelines.

SUMMARY

- With gas systems aboard a boat, the watchword is **safety**. Systems should be checked on a regular basis: pipework for corrosion, fittings and appliances for wear and joints for leaks. The gas system should be given a thorough service at least once every season.

- The rigging on a sailing yacht can make topsides maintenance much more arduous than that of a powerboat. The main things to ensure are that screws are tight and that anything that has come loose is tightened or replaced. Tracks and winches should receive regular attention if serviceability is to be maintained.

- Ropes are one of the main items of deck equipment on any boat. Cared for, they will give years of efficient service. Ensure that they are not kinked when being coiled, that they are clean and that the ends are sealed and whipped to prevent fraying.

7

THE POWER UNIT

The engine or engines are the means to move the boat; on a power boat they are perhaps the **only** means of moving it. (At least on a sailing yacht you have the opportunity of putting up a sail and using the power of the available wind to get you from port to port.) The power unit should be regarded as one of the most important parts of your boat's fabric. If engines are regularly maintained and looked after they will perform well and are unlikely to let you down at sea. Simple maintenance procedures should be carried out daily as a matter of course and good seamanship before a cruise commences: sump-oil level, stern-greaser and cooling-water levels should all be checked and topped up as required, but for long-term reliability the engines should be given a comprehensive service. The type of engine will vary and depend to some extent upon the type of boat you own. In general, engines are likely to be either inboard or outboard on a power boat, and probably a small auxiliary fitted with a sail drive leg on a sailing yacht.

Outboard Motors

Preventative maintenance should be the watchword to ensure engine reliability, and a comprehensive winter laying-up procedure (fully explained in Chapter 10) together with regular bouts of general servicing will reduce the chances of failure. The main requirements for outboard servicing are care and common-sense. The tools required are usually available in the average tool-box and will include a variety of spanners, sockets and screwdrivers of both types, as well as a set of feeler gauges, wire wool and adequate quantities of gearbox and sump oil. A waterproof grease and spray will also be required.

Before starting the service, remove the engine from the boat and take it home, supporting it on a ready-made outboard stand or on a sturdy plank of wood screwed to the workbench. This will allow you to work all around the engine without the need for constant lifting. A test tank made from an old oil drum filled three-quarters full with fresh water is also a good idea as an outboard engine should not be run out of water as this would cause rapid overheating and damage. An adequate source of light is a must for illuminating things, such as the carburettor and fuel lines; a multi-angle lamp is ideal for this purpose. A small torch is also useful here.

The basic service requirement of an outboard engine will remain the same from model to model, the only difference is whether the unit is two-stroke or four-stroke. With a two-stroke engine, it uses a combination of petrol and outboard engine oil, mixed in proportion as its combustible fuel, whereas a four-stroke engine is similar in operation to that of a car with a sump of oil for lubrication and separate petrol supply for the fuel. Ignition systems will also vary from engine to engine; most will use a magneto system driven off the flywheel to provide a spark for plugs and contact breaker, but some more up-to-date units are likely to incorporate special breakerless electronic ignition systems with no moving parts and which require little servicing.

Power Head Access

Access to the power head is usually achieved by removing the top cowl. This is held down with snap-off clips or a central screw. The spark plugs can be located easily on the power head and should be removed using a plug spanner. Inspect them, at regular intervals, especially if your motor is used on the canal system where slow trolling speeds might cause excessive oiling up. This is one of the big disadvantages of using a two-stroke on canals and rivers. Plugs should be changed after every 60 to 100 hours of engine running and the correct replacements fitted. For their numbers look in your engine handbook.

The correct electrode gap should be set using the feeler gauges. Each plug and engine will have a slightly different gap, but usually this will be in the region of 0.5–0.6mm (0.02–0.024in). For certain conditions engine performance and ignition might be improved by using a 'hotter' or 'cooler' type of plug. Usually a plug is too cold when carbon deposits build up on the white porcelain insulator and the plug tip becomes sooty or oily, while a plug that is too hot will show signs of white or cracked porcelain and a pitted or melted electrode. For further infor-

The spark plugs on the outboard motor should be removed and inspected for wear on a regular basis. New plugs should have their electrode gaps adjusted to the correct setting using feeler gauges.

mation on plug selection consult any manufacturer's application chart. Take care not to over-tighten the plugs when you replace them, as some engine blocks are made from alloys which will cause plug threads to strip if too much force is used. If possible, use a torque wrench adjusted to the correct torque setting for your engine.

Gearbox Oil

The lower leg of the outboard contains the bevelled gearing that transfers the drive from the vertical shaft to a horizontal mode before coupling to the propeller. The gears are encased in a jacket which is filled with oil. The oil should be changed every 100 hours of engine running by removing the two screws marked OIL FILL and DRAIN, letting the oil drip out into an old bowl and making sure that it is all ejected by turning the engine over gently a couple of times by hand after making sure the gear lever is in neutral. Refill the box through the bottom hole until it appears at the top one, replacing the screws and wiping off any spilled oil from the leg.

The fuel filter can usually be found in the fuel line between the inlet socket and the carburettor pump. Take off the securing clips or hose clamp then slacken the retaining nut on top of the filter body and lift it away. Take out the filter element, which may be a simple gauze ring or cup, and rinse it thoroughly in fresh, clean petrol. Rinse out the filter bowl and reassemble, refitting the sealing 'O' ring. Check fuel pipes, then prime the system and check for leaks.

Cooling Water

An important part of the outboard system is its cooling water supply. This is drawn in from the sea or river through a filter, then pumped around an internal jacket, so cooling the engine. You can tell if this water is actually circulating by a small tell-tale jet which should be constantly emitting water when the engine is running. If it stops or falters suspect that the intake port has become blocked with weed, mud or plastic bags. These should be removed to prevent overheating. On some outboards a small grille can be taken off to allow a finger or wood spill to be inserted to aid clearing. Many outboards now have a special flush plug attachment fitted to the lower leg which allows the connection of a hose-pipe. This should be used every time the motor has been used at sea to purge salt from the cooling jacket.

Propeller and Shaft

The propeller should be removed occasionally and checked for chipped or bent blades. Check the shaft for tangled bits of fishing line or rope and grease it using a suitable marine lubricant. Check the protective shear pin or splined rubber shock hub for wear, replacing as required. Galvanic corrosion on an outboard is prevented by a sacrificial anode fitted to the leg, usually below the anti-cavitation plate (the big flat plate above the propeller). Check it for signs of wear, fitting a new one if badly wasted.

While the top cowl is off, have a look at the pull-starter cord. This gets quite a lot of hard use, especially if the engine is difficult to start, and can suffer from fraying and wear. Pull the cord out slowly on its spring recoiler examining it along its length for signs of wear. I always carry a spare starter cord in the boat's tool-box in case the one on the motor breaks, but most outboards have a pulley set on top of the flywheel, around which a piece of stout cord can be wrapped to act as an emergency starter.

General Lubrication

Finally, all exposed moving parts and linkages should be given a blob of grease on a monthly basis. These parts include the swivel bracket, transom clamp screws, carburettor links and throttle and gear-change movements. Make sure that all steering connections are secure after replacing the motor on the boat, and ensure that the engine is correctly aligned in the centre of the transom and that the clamps are tight before starting. For extra security, a chain can be attached between the motor and the boat which will serve as a deterrent to thieves and prevent the motor from being dropped over the side when removing or replacing. A good tip is to tilt the motor out of the water every time it is stopped and out of use. This will help to prevent water from seeping into the lower leg. Always remember never to run the engine out of water otherwise damage will be caused to the water-pump impeller.

Over the Side!

The outboard motor sometimes does fall over the side, usually when it is being lifted on or off the boat. This is the time they are at their most vulnerable. They are heavy and cumbersome and difficult to lift off a transom-well or bracket which can cause the unthinkable to occur. It can mean the loss of the engine altogether, if it falls overboard in deep water at sea, or it might just mean a long wait for the tide to turn or a call out for the local diver. In any event, once the motor has been recovered, measures should be taken straightaway to prevent further, perhaps more serious damage from occurring.

Some of the smaller, lighter outboard motors can be taken home and cleaned up in the garage. However, many larger units will have to be done either near the boat or taken along to the nearest service centre for your make. Your owner's manual will give advice on this.

Many boat owners do in fact keep a small set of popular spare parts for their outboards aboard the boat along with the toolkit. Items such as spare spark plugs, high tension cable, fuel filter and oil, etc. can be of use in cleaning a motor that has been submerged. If it is impossible to get your unit to a service station, clean it up as best as you can, but do not attempt to start it up in case dirt has entered the cylinders along with water. This could seriously damage the motor with bent con rods

being the result. Of course, if you were unlucky enough to have lost the motor overboard while it was running, this could well be the case as water would in all probability have been sucked inside through the exhaust ports. Damage will then only be rectified after much more radical service work involving mechanical parts.

As soon as the immersed motor has been recovered from the water, stand it upright on the boat or quay to allow most of the water to drain naturally out of the power head and lower-leg assembly. Take off the fuel line to the remote tank or unscrew the filler cap to the outboard's own integral fuel tank. Drain off the fuel and any water that has entered the tank. The fuel tank should then be rinsed out with methylated spirits or carbon tetrachloride solution to purge the water fully, finally rinsing with

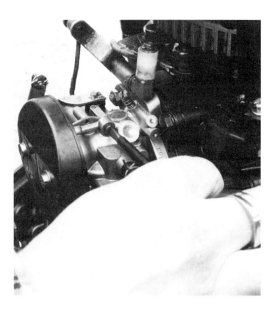

Adjusting the slow-running (trolling) setting on the carburettor of an outboard motor. Details of how this is done can usually be found in the owner's handbook supplied with the engine.

fresh fuel before draining out and allowing to dry.

Take off the carburettor (remembering how it was attached) and flush it out in the same way with fresh fuel. Tilt the engine to drain out any water from the cylinders. Taking out the spark plugs will also allow this to be done. Either wash the plugs or, better still, replace them with new ones of the correct type, not forgetting to re-gap them using feeler gauges.

Freshwater Wash

Wash down the entire motor with freshwater to remove salt deposits and dry it as best you can. A hair-dryer can be used sparingly here to speed up the process. Take off the flywheel and wash and dry the coils, magneto and points (which will probably require replacement). You should also replace the HT cables.

A light machine oil should be squirted into the cylinders (about 1 teaspoonful) and the motor turned over by hand using the flywheel to distribute the oil. A squirt of the same oil should be given to the fuel-inlet manifold. At this point the smooth running of the pistons in the bores should be ascertained. All should run very freely; if there are tight spots it means that water or dirt, or both, has got into the cylinders and the motor will need professionally servicing, so contact your local dealer.

Once the above cleaning schedule has been completed, the motor may be started up to check on running. Replace all parts removed, including the flywheel, and check for any wetness remaining in the ignition circuit. A spray over with WD40 should help prevent spark stray. Oil the spark plug threads if using the old plugs and refit them to the engine. Do not over-tighten (use a torque wrench if available).

Put some fresh fuel/oil mixture into the tank or reconnect the fuel line to the remote tank. For this initial run allow twice the amount of oil you would usually use. For example 100:1 becomes 50:1 and so on. Start up the motor either by cord or electric start and run on about one-quarter throttle for 30 seconds or so, just to ensure that it has not in fact seized. It is best to run the motor on the boat in the water and quite hard until it warms up thoroughly. The heat generated will soon dry out any water left behind in the power head and on the ignition circuitry.

If the motor fails to start after checking that everything is back in place, consult your service dealer and take no chances!

Prevention is better than cure, so lash the motor to the boat with a safety chain or stout rope from an eye bolt in the transom to the ring which can be found in the castings of most makes of outboard.

Inboard Engines

To cope with the strains of high-speed running for hours at a time, the marine inboard engine is designed to be tough, with many parts strengthened to withstand the pounding it will receive from choppy conditions, heavy weather and the salt-laden environment into which it has been installed. The main requirements for trouble-free operation are regular maintenance, an adequate cooling water system and clean fuel. It therefore follows that the fuel system and cooling water supply should be given more than a cursory examination at maintenance time. The ignition system is also prone to defects if not regularly checked. It should be cleaned and adjusted, pitted contact breakers removed and replaced, spark

The modern inboard engine is a complex unit, but simple servicing and daily checks can be done by the owner with a modicum of knowledge and some basic spares and tools.

plugs cleaned and adjusted, and high-tension cables fully waterproofed. To do these jobs, it is essential to have an adequate toolkit, a selection of spare parts for the engine and a sound knowledge of the areas you will be working on. For this, there is no better way than to obtain a full workshop manual for your engine which will show greater detail than your engine handbook. The manual should be kept aboard the boat as it may be required to help effect repairs while at sea or in a remote area, away from immediate help.

Diesel Fuel Systems

The fuel system of a diesel engine is simple enough to understand. Basically, it comprises a main fuel storage tank with filler tube, cap and vent situated some-where convenient at deck level, a water-stop filter to take out any droplets of water that have inadvertently contaminated the diesel (perhaps when filling up in the rain), a sedimenter, which has a low resistance to the fuel, and that separates particles of water the water stop has missed, together with solid matter, into a special deposit bowl at its base. Next comes the main lift pump, worked from the engine and used to supply fuel to the injectors, the filter agglomerator, which is used to remove small particles of dirt plus any remaining water and finally the main filter which removes anything that the previous items have missed. As you can see, pure, clean fuel is vital to the sound running of the engine.

Removing the oil filter on a diesel engine is a job that should be done once at the start of the cruising season and again when the boat is laid up for the winter.

One of the main reasons for all this filtration is not just the prevention of dirt and water (no fuel should be that dirty) but the prevention of minute particles of abrasive material from reaching and damaging the very accurate components of the engine's injection system. The injectors are manufactured to high tolerances and, like fuel pumps, have specially mated parts which are put together in the factory with immense care. This is one of the reasons why boat owners should never attempt to service them themselves. They should always be sent away to the manufacturer for service and repairs.

There are, however, several things that the owner can do. Every week or so, prior to starting the engines, drain off any accumulated water or sediment from the water stop and sedimenter by unscrewing the small drain plugs which can be found under the collecting bowl at the base. A small plastic cup held beneath the unit will prevent gunge from falling into the bilge and will allow you to see just how much, if any, fuel contamination you have. If there is quite a lot of water and dirt, you may have a leaking deck filler or fractured supply pipe or gasket and this should be checked and repaired straight away.

The fuel agglomerator can be checked and drained off in the same way and its filter element replaced once every season. This is usually done in conjunction with the main fuel filter element at laying-up time in the autumn and the procedure is explained below.

Fuel Filter

It is worth wiping over the whole filter assembly before you begin work to remove any dirt or grime that might contaminate the inner workings once you have stripped them down. Turn off the fuel at the stop cock before dismantling and drain off any fuel from the filter bowl into a cup via the drain screw. Next, unscrew the central bolt of the filter assembly, holding the base of the filter to prevent it from turning. The base section will then drop downwards into your hand with a short pull.

Remove and discard the old filter element and take out the three rubberized sealing rings that are fitted in the grooves in the top, base and centre. Clean out the inside of the base and filter top using a clean, dry cloth which does not leave a fluffy deposit, or a small, clean paintbrush. Fit the new sealing rings which will be supplied with your filter set. Depending upon which type of filter you have, the rings may be of slightly different diameters, so check this fact when you take out the old ones. When installing the new rings, make sure that they are seated correctly in the grooves without kinking.

The next job is to fit the new filter element into the base, making sure that the larger of the steel rims of the element is uppermost. Offer the complete base and element up to the filter head, rotating the element so that it slides over the central 'O' ring. Complete the job by tightening the central bolt, being careful not to over-tighten. If you have a torque wrench a setting of about 1 kg/m (7–8 lb/ft) should be sufficient. Finally, turn on the fuel at the cock and proceed to bleed the air from the system as per the instructions in your engine handbook.

Regularly check for leaks in the fuel line, indicated by dribbles of diesel around joints or unions. Check that your fuel pipes are properly clipped at regular intervals otherwise they will soon fatigue under vibration and either break or let in air. Check too, the condition of your fuel shut-off valves which should ideally be positioned near the cockpit where they can be easily reached.

Petrol Fuel Systems

The fuel system on a petrol or gasoline engine needs little in the way of servicing, except to check the filters for cleanliness, occasionally flushing them out with fresh petrol. On many engines there will be a small sight glass which indicates that the fuel lines are full and the fuel pump operating correctly. This should also be removed for cleaning, flushing out any

sediment that has collected in the bottom. A visual check of the fuel line, pipes and unions, etc. will show whether there are any leaks which should be repaired immediately. It is bad enough to have a fuel leak on a diesel engine, let alone on a petrol one with its more volatile fuel!

Petrol Ignition Systems

The ignition system on a petrol engine will hold few mysteries for those boat owners who are familiar with the basic workings of the family car. They are basically very similar in their operation but both require the same amount of regular attention and servicing.

Almost every marine engine manu-facturer offers a complete range of petrol engines alongside his diesel units and many boats are taking advantage of the higher power outputs and much lower power to weight ratios offered. The ignition system is fairly simple to under-stand and to service. Parts required include a set of sparking plugs, a new contact breaker set, and possibly a new set of ignition leads and distributor cap, depending upon the length of time these items have been in service. Most of the parts can be easily obtained from your local motoring accessory shop, but in the case of some engines specialized parts may have to be purchased direct from a marine engine supplier.

The ignition circuit is very simple with a rotor arm operating from a cam-driven crankshaft. Some modern engines might even have done away with this system, as with some outboard motors, and will be using a closed electronic ignition instead. This unit will be unserviceable and will come as a replacement item obtainable from your engine service and spares dealer.

Battery

The best place to start is with the engine starter battery. Check that it is fully charged with plenty of power available to turn over the engine. Check the battery installation, greasing terminals and make sure that the battery is well lashed down in its box. The ignition coil can usually be left well alone as it normally functions well without trouble for years on end. A spray over with WD40 will keep water and damp at bay, and the continuity of the coil can be checked by bridging its primary windings with a test lamp of 12 volts attached to a couple of wires. If the bulb glows when the points are closed, the coil is working.

The secondary windings of the coil and the main high-tension lead going to the distributor cap can be checked by removing the lead at the distributor, clamping it in an insulator (a wooden clothes peg will do), and holding it about 6mm (¼in) from the block. If the engine is now turned over a bright blue spark should be produced across the gap.

Examine the distributor cap itself and check for traces of carbon tracking caused by a build-up of carbon and dirt and which could cause the spark to be diverted away from where it is needed. The engine will probably work even if this occurs, but during a damp winter morning you might have difficulty in starting it. Once again, WD40 should cure the trouble. Once the cap and leads have been checked, replace or reset the contact-breaker gap by using a screwdriver and a set of feeler gauges. The correct gap will be found in your engine handbook. Ensure that the faces of the points are clean and free from pitting.

The rotor arm, which is also covered by the distributor cap, should be examined to see that its spring has not gone weak. This spring is important as it transfers the high-tension current to all sparking plugs.

The plugs themselves should be removed, using a proper plug spanner, and checked for signs of overheating which usually shows up in a burnt electrode and cracked porcelain insulator. It is always better to replace them at a major service, fitting the correct types (reference number on the side) and setting the correct electrode gap with the feeler gauges. Finally, clean off the top end of the engine, removing grime and oil.

Cooling Systems

The cooling water that flows around the internal jacket of your engine is, like the oil, a lifeblood keeping the engine running at its optimum temperature for maximum performance and minimum wear and tear.

There are several types of cooling system that can be fitted to marine engines, those cooled by the surrounding air, those into which fresh water is circulated from a separate header tank in an enclosed system and those engines that are cooled by raw water being taken from outside the boat directly from the river, canal or sea.

The simplest form of cooling has to be air-cooling and in these models you will note that there will be no water pumps, heat exchangers and thermostats. You will probably also notice the increased noise coming from an air-cooled engine. It is important to keep the ducting pipes clean and free from blockage, the vent grilles clear on the exterior part of the hull, and the cooling fins on the power head should also be kept clean to allow the free flow of cooling air.

Fan-belt Tension

The main fan should also be periodically checked for blade splits, looseness and wear and the drive belt checked for wear and slackness. Carry a spare belt amongst your boat tools and parts box.

Inlet Filter

If you operate your boat in mainly shallow conditions, such as those found in estuaries or rivers, you will need to check regularly the inlet filters for sand, mud or silt deposits. Even with filters a certain amount of grit will find its way into the internal jacket of the engine and this must be flushed away if overheating is to be avoided. The problem here is greatest at smaller bore areas around the exhaust manifold and the cylinder head. A high-pressure water hose can be used for this job, and some engines even have a special attachment point for this.

The freshwater pump, which is usually belt driven but can occasionally be driven from a moving part of the engine like the camshaft, should require very little main-tenance. The bearings are usually packed with grease and are sealed for life. Noisy or leaking pumps should probably be replaced but with some popular types a new bearing kit may be available. Sea-water pumps are also very simple in their construction and operation, basically consisting of a casting with an inlet and outlet port, inspection plate, seal and rubber impeller. This type of pump can be checked for leaks when running. The usual place will be near the inspection plate seal which will almost certainly be damaged. This must be replaced.

Impeller

With the cover removed from the pump, coat the impeller with a waterproof grease which will help movement, especially if the engine has not been used for several weeks. If the impeller looks worn or the rubber perished, replace it immediately and always carry a spare one in the boat's tool-box. If a blade breaks off the impeller and drops down into the cooling pipework it must be located otherwise overheating from blockage may result.

Do not forget to inhibit the engine cooling system during the winter months. If you use the boat all year round, put the correct amount of antifreeze into a closed water-cooling system in order to protect it from the ravages of winter weather. The rule with engine cooling systems is check regularly for leaks from pipes and pumps, look for blockages in inlet filters and regularly service your fresh- and sea-water pumps.

General Engine Checks

Check the condition of water pumps and belts, retensioning as required. Change the sump oil and filter and check the security of all hose and pipe clips on fuel lines and the cooling water system. Give the various grease nipples and lubrication points their due amount of the correct grades of grease and oil and check the security of the steering and control linkages. Once a year, usually at laying-up time, the engine should be degreased to remove dirt and grime, and any chipped paintwork touched up. Ensure that the bilges are clean and dry and that the bilge pump is operating.

The Outdrive Leg

One part of the engine and its transmission that is easily forgotten, until it goes wrong, is that big lump that hangs on the transom, the outdrive!

There are now several different types of outdrive available from a range of manufacturers, such as Mercruiser and Volvo Penta, together with a smaller number of specialist units that can be fitted to a variety of inboard engines, like the Enfield and Sonic drives. The general construction is much the same; a large cast case that holds the special gearing that transmits the drive from the engine gearbox from a horizontal mode down through the vertical and back to the horizontal again.

Bellows

One of the more important parts to check is the rubber boot or bellows that covers the hull joint and any associated exhaust system. Check for perishing of the rubber, or leaks of hydraulic fluid. The bellows are reasonably simple to replace and are usually held in place with clamping clips. Spares are available from the engine manufacturer or from a whole host of country-wide dealers. One word of advice though, try to ensure that you only buy a genuine spare part. There are some inferior types available, but this goes with most marine equipment. You only get what you pay for, but with an engine it always pays to buy the best.

The techniques involved with servicing an outdrive are similar in many respects to those employed when servicing the lower end of a standard outboard engine. The gear case will be lubricated in a similar way and must be drained off occasionally and

Taking off the cap from the lower gearbox to inspect the rubber seal. If, on draining out the gearbox oil, water comes out with it, the seal should be suspected and replaced.

refilled with the correct replacement oil. Usually this is done via a drain screw at the bottom of the leg and a filling screw near the top. Check the condition of the sacrificial anode which will be bolted to the lower leg on the anticavitation plate (the flat plate just above the propeller). If it is badly wasted it should be replaced. On some newer models of outdrive the anode will be in the form of a circular collar which is behind the propeller. Again, replacements can be had from your engine dealer.

Propeller

Check the propeller itself. Is it bent out of

Removing the propeller from an outdrive leg in order to grease the shaft and remove any fishing line and debris that may have become entangled.

but on average expect to pay around £75 – £100 for a regrind, tip replacement and reshaping. With a very old prop it might even be worth replacing it with a new one.

While the propeller is removed, check that the shaft is free from nylon fishing line or rope which can wrap itself tightly around and go unnoticed. Don't forget to replace the prop shaft drive pin with a brand new one and lubricate the shaft with a waterproof light grease, such as Duckhams Keenol.

Paintwork

Finally, any damage to the paintwork should be touched up using an appropriate enamel paint as recommended by the engine manufacturer. Do not just use any old paint as a colour match will be unlikely and you could end up doing more damage. Remember not to paint over the anode and don't use any form of antifouling on the lower leg.

shape or are the tips of the blades badly chipped or worn? If so, this will affect the performance of your boat in the water, and an out-of-balance propeller can cause an undue amount of vibration which can rapidly wear out oil seals and the prop shaft itself. Propellers can be removed and sent away to one of the many prop refurbishers now in business. The cost of this will depend on the state of the prop,

Ensure that all the actions of the leg are operating smoothly; swivel, tilt mechanism, gear change and steering. There is very little else to do. If a general eye is kept on the leg throughout the cruising season and the above tips are done at laying-up time, your outdrive should give you years of reliable and trouble-free service.

SUMMARY

- The engine is the heart of the boat. Without it you go nowhere and cannot produce electricity to run your equipment. It should be regularly serviced once a year and checked on a daily basis during the cruising season.

- Outboard motors are best serviced away from the boat at home. Mount the unit on a plank screwed to the workbench or on a special outboard stand to make service access easier. An old oil drum filled three-quarters full with fresh water will serve as a running tank.

- On outdrive legs and outboard motors, check the condition of the special sacrificial anode that protects the leg from the ravages of galvanic corrosion. If badly wasted it should be replaced.

8

CORROSION

Whatever material your boat is made of, some parts of it will inevitably be subject to attack by corrosion. Steel boats will immediately spring to mind as being top of the corrosion list but this is not necessarily always the case. If steel boats are properly prepared and protected from new by grit blasting and epoxy painting, they will be less prone to corrosion and general deterioration than a timber or glass-fibre boat. Corrosion appears in various forms, the most obvious and visible being rust which is brought about by the biodegradable nature of steel. Rust is simply iron oxide caused by steel returning to its natural state.

Electrolytic Corrosion

Electrolytic corrosion is caused by stray currents from badly made electrical connections and installations and the result of this is that any metal immersed in sea water, which has the effect of earthing the current, will be quickly and seriously corroded. This is one very good reason for always switching off the main battery isolating switches when leaving the boat unattended for a period of time. In fact, the only circuit which should be left 'live' is the one supplying the bilge pump automatic float switch which ensures that water does not build up when no one is aboard. It is to be hoped that any current is then prevented from straying.

Galvanic Corrosion

The cocktail of dissimilar metals and sea water is a volatile one. Most metals will corrode to some extent when immersed into a fresh- or salt-water solution for a period of time and on a boat this applies in general to such items as the propeller, stern gear, outboard engine, sterndrive legs and even the hull itself if it is made from steel plate.

The problem of galvanic corrosion is caused by a small but significant electrical current flowing between the water (electrolyte) and the metals involved (anodes and cathodes). This, in effect, is the way in which a wet battery works. (In some severe cases enough current will be produced to light a small bulb!) In producing this current one of the metals will become seriously corroded.

Most impure metals, specially brass and other alloys, such as copper, are susceptible because they contain particles in their make-up that are either positive or negative. When immersed into a conductive medium, such as the sea or badly polluted freshwater, a small cell or battery is formed, causing current to flow from the anode or base metal to the cathode or more noble metal. To understand this effect we must look at the galvanic scale which includes all metals and places them in positions relative to each other within the scale. The table of metals in the galvanic

101

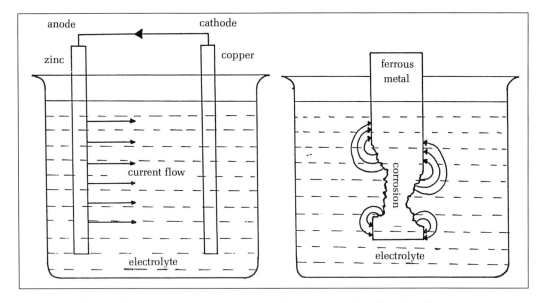

When dissimilar metals, such as copper, bronze or steel are immersed in a liquid, such as sea water, a small electrical battery or cell is formed. Small electric currents will flow from the anode to the cathode causing the anode to corrode away.

series shows the susceptibility of certain metals to corrosion. You will notice that the more NOBLE metals at the top of the scale are less likely to corrode than the softer or BASE metals at the bottom end which will corrode at a much greater rate. The further apart the metals are on the scale, the greater the likelihood of the base metal corroding when the two are brought into contact in sea water.

The Galvanic Scale

This scale covers most of the common metals used in the construction and operation of boats today.

Graphite
Platinum
Stainless steel type 316
Stainless steel type 304
Silver
Lead
Gunmetal
Silicon bronze
Manganese bronze
Copper
Tin
Brass
Aluminium bronze
Mild Steel
Aluminium alloy
Zinc
Magnesium

It is worth noting that graphite is right at the top of the scale which makes it imperative never to use any graphite grease for lubrication anywhere on the boat as this will lead to rapid corrosion of any underwater metals that it comes into contact with. This is especially important in the area around the propeller, stern gear, rudder and shaft assemblies or outdrive leg.

Sea Cocks

There are many items of equipment on the glass-fibre boat which need checking and care to prevent corrosion from occurring. Sea cocks are particularly prone to failure through the effects of corrosion, with gate valves refusing to open or close and even valve tops shearing off in use. There are so many grades of metal from which sea cocks are made that it is difficult, if not impossible, for the boat owner to know for certain whether the shiny item he is buying over the chandler's counter is in fact a proper marine-grade cock of gunmetal or a much cheaper brass model from the local plumbers.

Cheap brass and manganese bronze fittings will suffer from dezincification (the dissolving of the zinc content from the brass) when immersed into sea water. This will eventually lead to the failure of the fitting, with disastrous consequences as the remaining spongy copper has little inherent strength. It is also worth using the correct grade of metal below the water-line to prevent this problem occurring.

It surprises many people to learn that stainless steel is far from suitable for underwater use as it suffers from its own form of corrosion. For instance, if a barnacle attaches itself to a piece of underwater stainless steel, the surface of the steel becomes starved of oxygen and the oxide layer which is vital to the metal's corrosion resistance begins to fail. When this happens a galvanic cell is set up and corrosion of the underlying surface takes place, resulting in pitting and a gradual loss of strength in the item. This type of corrosion is not all that easy to spot in its final stages. All that can be done is to give each item a regular inspection, looking out for signs of pitting, corrosion etc.

Outboards and Sterndrive Legs

Equally at risk are outboard motor and sterndrive lower leg units which are cast from aluminium and suffer particularly badly from the effects of corrosion. Propeller shafts, 'P' and 'A'-type support brackets and metal rudders can also suffer and need to be checked occasionally to gauge whether corrosive forces are at work. A good system is to check the boat below the water-line after the first season's use and then every two years after that if all appears to be in order.

With a basic understanding of the process of galvanic corrosion it becomes easier to avoid causing corrosion problems by not making the mistake of bolting stainless steel rudders to aluminium outdrives or similar mismatches of metals. Having said this, there is also a relationship between the size of dissimilar metals and their corrosive potency. For instance, outboard motors and outdrives are assembled using stainless steel bolts which, at first glance, would appear to be a recipe for corrosion but, in fact, due to the vastly greater area of aluminium compared to stainless steel, the corrosion effect is more or less overwhelmed and corrosion becomes so slight as to be negligible.

Sacrificial Anodes

The usual method of protecting your metal parts from galvanic corrosion is to fit commercially available zinc anodes. These come in a variety of shapes and sizes for different applications and are fitted to the exterior of the hull, the rudder blade, outdrive leg, outboard engine cavitation plate and stern gear, etc. The zinc, being

very low on the galvanic scale, is very corrosive and is attacked by the other metals, corroding before they do.

Glass-fibre or wooden boats fitted with anodes must have internal bonding to each item to be protected so that everything is interlinked and in contact with the anodic system. This is usually done internally by strapping the anodes to the various fittings using large gauge conductors and cable. Anodes on glass-fibre and wooden boats that are not internally bonded are totally useless and will offer no protection. It is also essential to ensure that anodes are never painted over as this also prevents them from working.

Apart from the engine and stern gear, all the sea cocks, inlet valves and water-intake ports should be protected by their own

For the maximum protection of underwater metal parts, anodes of various sizes can be fitted. Here a small round anode has been installed on the steel bilge keels of this sailing cruiser.

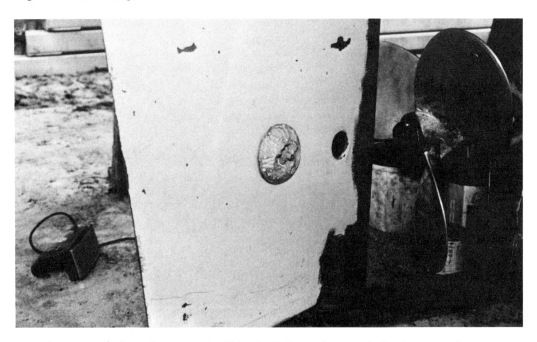

After about one year of use, the anodes should be checked to see how much they have wasted. This anode, fitted to a rudder, has become partially corroded but should last at least one more year before replacement becomes necessary.

individual anodes, bonded electrically to each other. If you are unsure about the type of anodes to buy for your particular boat, contact one of the main suppliers of cathodic protection devices, such as M. G. Duff or Vetus, who will be able to supply you with more detailed information.

Regular Inspection

Once the anodes have been fitted, many boat owners tend to forget about them. This is fatal as anodes should be inspected at least once a year, usually at lay-up time when the craft is slipped from the water. If the anode is more than about 20 per cent wasted it should be replaced. If more than this amount, check on the bonding of the

anode to the metal it is supposed to be protecting as you might have a break in continuity. If the anodes remain clean and uncorroded they are not working.

Outboards and outdrives usually come fitted with their own anodes in the form of a small zinc slab bolted to the cavitation plate or under the leg somewhere. On certain sterndrive units, such as Mercruiser or Volvo Penta, the anode comes in the form of a zinc collar which is fitted behind the propeller and this requires the removal of the prop in order to change it.

Engine blocks, too, might be protected with small zinc plugs, which have a short screw thread protruding from the end, and which are screwed into special ports on the engine blocks. It is a simple matter to check and change this type of anode.

SUMMARY

- Any boat that has different metals used in its construction, especially on underwater equipment like the rudder or propeller shaft, is liable to galvanic corrosion if not properly protected by self-sacrificing zinc or magnesium anodes.

- Once the anodes have been fitted to the various parts requiring protection, continuity should be ensured by bonding each item to its neighbour using sturdy cables.

- Inspect your anodes at least once a year, especially if your boat is kept afloat all season. Replace them if they are about three-quarters wasted. If, after one year, the anodes are still in pristine condition, they are not doing their job!

9
BUYING SECOND-HAND BOATS

Unless you have the means to go out and buy a brand new boat outright, you will probably be in the position of choosing a second-hand model. Perhaps the new craft available do not suit your own particular requirements as they may be too small, too powerful or too expensive. The second-hand boat market usually has an excellent selection of many types and varieties of boat and most people usually find just what they are looking for there. There are however, one or two things that should be borne in mind before you rush out and part with your hard-earned cash.

Buying a second-hand glass-fibre boat can be a somewhat risky business unless you are fully prepared and aware of all the possible pitfalls. This chapter has been designed to help you to plan your inspection of a particular boat and either to recognize possible areas which may require attention before or after you buy, or to decide when the boat is so bad that you will leave it well alone. It takes the form of a simple and basic survey which the potential purchaser can carry out himself.

The prospect of purchasing a boat, whether new or second-hand, is exciting as one anticipates experiencing all the pleasures that boating brings. But buying a second-hand boat requires some fore-thought and it will be better, in the long run to have some idea of the problems which can occur with the older, used boat. How serious are these problems? Can they can be economically repaired, or should the boat be rejected as a bad buy? In making these decisions a good deal will depend on your ability to carry out your own repairs. This will determine what condition a boat needs to be in before you can consider buying it. Obviously a very tatty boat will sell for a much smaller figure than one in pristine condition and, where money is a prime consideration, this may mean that a potentially better and larger boat could be within your price range if you are prepared to accept extra renovation work.

These days there is almost no fault or repair work that cannot be tackled by the amateur, given sufficient time, money and enthusiasm, but care should be taken when considering a boat requiring large amounts of work. The finished job might have become so costly and time-consuming that it will have become un-economical, with the final bill exceeding the cost of a similar craft requiring little or no work.

Most small craft will be of glass fibre construction, although there are some wooden boats still around that are serving their owners well. The faults concerning GRP are, however, much less obvious than those affecting wooden craft which encompass a whole different set of rules for their care and repair.

Osmosis

One of the biggest problems facing glass-fibre craft today is that of osmotic blistering. This is dealt with in more detail in Chapter 4, but basically osmosis is caused by a variety of means during the construction stage and appears to affect modern boats slightly more than older models. It is also more of a problem for boats moored in freshwater rather than salt water.

The signs of osmosis are a blistering of the gel-coat layer below the water-line. If a blister is pricked a fluid escapes which can have a distinctive vinegary smell. It is caused when a fluid of a lower density (the water in which the boat floats) is drawn through a porous membrane (the gel-coat layer of the hull) to a fluid of a higher density (the void within the hull contains fluid of a higher density). The voids or holes within the hull are created by air bubbles not purged during the laying-up process. They often contain fluids such as curing agents and other substances used in the initial construction of the boat. If the problem is not too widespread it can be successfully treated and repaired by the DIY enthusiast, although the materials are costly and the process time-consuming. If you are thinking of doing repairs yourself, refer to the instructions given on pages 55–63. It will be wise only to consider taking on a boat in this condition if the selling price is attractive enough to reflect the remedial work required.

The port side stern quarter of this boat has had a bash that has broken off the fendering and damaged the superstructure moulding. It will obviously require repairs which will affect the selling price.

General Defects

Apart from osmosis there are several other less drastic problems which occur to GRP craft but which are more easily repaired. One of these is star crazing which appears as a series of hairline cracks often radiating out from a central point in a star formation. These are caused by the boat striking a hard object which stresses the hull skin, or a bulkhead or internal piece of furniture being fitted too tightly during the building stage which sets up internal stresses, cracking the gel coat over a period of time. A mud weight or heavy anchor dropped on the deck can have a similar effect, a badly placed chock, supporting the boat on a trailer or cradle can also cause distortion of the hull, leading to similar cracks. When the problem occurs on side decks it is usually

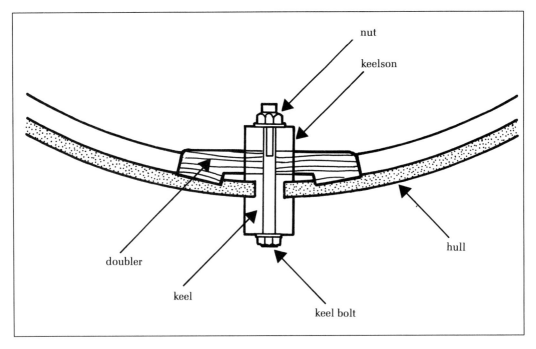

nut

keelson

hull

doubler

keel

keel bolt

The area around the keel should be inspected for signs of rusting which might mean corrosion of the keel bolts. If suspected, the keel can be X-rayed where bolts and metal fittings will be shown up.

due to insufficient support having been built in below, which allows excess flexing. The problem is usually quite easy to spot when you are examining the boat, but check the underlying surface. If this is still firm and shows no signs of sponginess due to water having entered the mat/resin matrix, then repairs should be simple enough still to make the boat a viable proposition.

When checking the hull, look out for cracking around the keel band or bilge keel fastenings which may have to be taken off to effect a repair. Also look for wear on strakes which will indicate whether the boat has been regularly dragged across a beach for launching. If the gel coat has actually worn away or been chipped right through, check again for sponginess in the underlying areas before deciding whether to buy and attempt a repair.

One good method of visually checking the hull is to put your eye close to it at one end and scan along the length. This usually shows up any imperfections quite clearly. Another way is to run your hands along the hull when it may be possible to feel any undulations or large areas where repair work may have been carried out.

The outboard well is another place where stress cracks can appear, especially around the clamp screws which attach the outboard engine to the boat. Rubbing bands should also be checked as their condition will give a good indication as to how much use the boat has had during its lifetime.

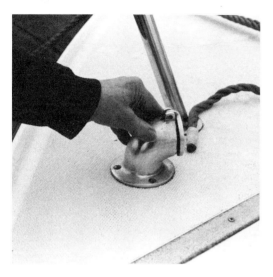

Examine deck fittings such as chain pipes, cleats, stanchions, fairleads, etc. for security. A good tug will show up any loose or badly strained fittings.

Deck fittings, which include fairleads, bollards, mooring posts and sea-rail stanchions, are all areas which require a thorough check. The bases of stanchions should be especially checked as a good deal of leverage is put upon them by people grabbing onto the upright and heaving themselves aboard. The bases should be reinforced by strong backing plates, preferably made of plywood and bonded to the underside of the deck with glass-fibre resin and mat. Check the type of fastenings that have been used: they should be good-quality bolts. The method used to check the sturdiness of a stanchion is to hold the top while moving it from side to side and front to back. Watch the deck near the stanchion base. If it flexes more than a very small amount, strengthening and reinforcement will be needed.

The timber capping on this cruiser has sprung away exposing the joint between hull and superstructure. It can be repaired easily but how much water has seeped into the joint in the meantime? Check around the area on the inside of the boat for signs of damp and staining of timber or other fittings.

109

When examining the interior of the boat, take up the floorboards and check the state of the bilges. They should have been painted out, which will help to prevent water from seeping into the glass-fibre laminate, as this picture clearly shows.

Inside the Hull

Moving inside the hull, if the bilges are bare glass fibre and have never been painted, expect to find signs of water ingress into the mat and resin matrix. If left unchecked, this will eventually weaken the hull structure and make the boat a very poor buy. Even where the bilges are well painted check all around the stringers and cross members for signs of movement or softness, although if only localized problems exist these can be repaired, but again only if the asking price is right.

Internal bulkheads and furniture which have been permanently bonded into position should be carefully examined to ensure that the areas where they are bonded in are sound and show no signs of breaking away from the hull or superstructure skin. If the bonding is breaking away from the timber bulkhead this usually indicates that damp has penetrated the woodwork and has crept behind the glass-fibre bonding. If the bonding is actually breaking away from the hull this usually means that some physical damage has occurred at some time in the past. Either problem is repairable if the damaged is localized, although rot may have set in to any areas of woodwork which have been subjected to long periods of damp, and this may necessitate the complete replacement of the panel.

Windows which leak are more than just a nuisance as they can lead to the type of damp problems which eventually lead to rot, so check for signs of water staining around the inside of window frames, whether they are made of rubber, aluminium or wood. Rubber window seals have a relatively short life but are cheap and easy to replace with the simple tool supplied by rubber manufacturers. If the window rubbers are in poor condition or if perspex windows have turned opaque, due to the effects of continual exposure to sunlight, both can be easily replaced.

While checking for water damage look in those areas where the deck fittings are bolted through as these will often let in water after a few years, especially on items such as cleats which occasionally come under high pressure from tight mooring lines and which can eventually start to work loose. As we have said, all this type of fitting should have stout internal backing pads, preferably glassed over for greater strength to reinforce the area of the deck where they are fitted.

Canopies

Cockpit canopies suffer with age but can be replaced at reasonable cost depending upon their size and complexity. Canopy windows, usually made of flexible clear plastic are more easily replaced at a fraction of the cost of a complete new canopy, so carefully check the condition of the canopy and its fittings, including the studs and hooks on the glass-fibre superstructure.

Engines

A glance in the engine compartment will usually tell you how the engines have been looked after. If the engine is covered in a film of oil with pools of water and grime lying under the engine and over its mounts, you can usually assume that the installation has been badly taken care of. A clean, tidy engine bay with pipework and electrical wiring clipped up and bilges free of spilled oil and water will indicate that regular servicing has taken place. A good pointer is to check if the hatch is easy to lift. If it is stuck down with dirt and has rusting hinges you can bet it has not been lifted for some time. Remember to check the condition of the fuel tank, especially outboard tanks which are prone to corrosion.

Once you have completed your own inspection on the lines laid out above, now will be the time to negotiate a price for the boat with the vendor but only 'subject to survey'. It is important to state this as it is a safeguard against making a legally binding agreement to buy a boat that may, in fact, be unsound when given a thorough examination by a professional surveyor.

Cockpit canopies are very prone to damage, usually to the perspex windows. If the main canopy is intact, the windows can be replaced for a relatively small cost.

Electrical System

The electrical system on a small boat is generally a fairly simple affair so should not cause too many problems, but it will be worth checking the system to see what type of connections have been used at terminal points under the dashboard, and at the back of gauges, etc. The fuse-box should also be examined, looking out for wires that have been just twisted together and taped over which may indicate that the previous owner has not been particularly fastidious in the care and maintenance of his craft. If this is the case the entire electrical system will need careful checking and, if necessary, rewiring using proper crimp terminals, the correct gauge of cable and proper fittings. All these things are freely available and the task is not complex.

The main engine starter and domestic

storage batteries should be checked for general condition and should be mounted securely in their boxes or housings to prevent movement when under way at sea. Are the battery terminals tight and free of corrosive substances?

The Professional Surveyor

Now is the time to call in the professional marine surveyor who will inspect the boat and make a full written report, detailing the condition of all aspects from the hull to the electrical system. This report can be quite useful when it comes to dealing with insurance companies or financial bodies who might insist on it before granting insurance or releasing money for purchase. Many insurance companies will only require a surveyor's report on a boat that is over ten years old, but it will be worth telling the surveyor that you want the report and a possible valuation before he carries out the work.

Because the cost of employing a surveyor can be quite high (including travelling expenses as well as time), it will be best to ensure that you have done most of the groundwork and initial inspection of the boat yourself. In this way you will be fairly sure that the boat is definitely the one you want and that you will not be booking the surveyor to view several boats, one after the other. You should narrow down your choice to the one craft so that on the day the surveyor calls, it will be really only to confirm that you have missed nothing serious and to give you his written report. Remember that once you have agreed a price with the vendor, you have a legal obligation to complete the sale unless, of course, the survey shows up something really disastrous!

SUMMARY

- These days there is almost no fault or repair work that cannot be tackled by the amateur, given sufficient time, money and enthusiasm, but care should be taken when considering buying a boat requiring so much work that the finished job may well end up costing more than a similar boat in good condition.

- When checking a hull, look out for cracking around the keel band or bilge keel fastenings which may have to be taken off to effect a repair. Also sight along the hull sides which will give an indication of bad distortion and possible internal problems.

- When you have tracked down the boat you want to buy, call in a professional surveyor who will inspect the boat and make a full written report, detailing the condition of all aspects of the craft from hull to electrical system.

10

PUTTING THE BOAT TO BED

At the end of the useful cruising season, in the UK this usually means the end of September or mid-October, the boat, if it is not to be used throughout the winter months, should be prepared for its period of inactivity either at the marina, boatyard or on the drive at home. Even in the warmer climates a boat will need to be removed from the water for occasional repair, cleaning and painting work and this is best done at the end of the year. A good many boat owners do nothing when they have finished using their boat during summer, simply leaving it to the rigours of winter weather without so much as a thought as to the effects this will have on upon the fabric of the boat, its engine and equipment. The shocks that await these owners who return at the start of the new season can include floods from burst water systems left undrained, blown core plugs on engines not wintered, split copper piping on water systems and, in some extreme cases, boats left half sunk from sea cocks left open. All this is guaranteed to have a lasting effect on the nerves of the individual as well as his bank balance!

Wintering the craft is an essential part of boat ownership and the steps taken to prepare a boat for winter will be handsomely repaid with trouble-free cruising the following year. Before starting work, sit down for an hour on the boat with a pad of paper and pencil and make a list of things to do. Look at each section of the boat in turn: the hull, the deck and superstructure, the engine, the electrical system, the water system and the ancillary equipment. The work that is necessary should then be split into the jobs that can be done aboard the boat, those that can be taken away to be done at home and those that will have to be completed by the boatyard. When looking over the boat, imagine, if you like, that you are looking at her for the first time with a view to buying. In this way, you will notice all the things that require attention, from the flaking paintwork, the scratches and dents in the hull, the navigation lights that no longer work, the frayed and tatty warps, damaged rigging and spars and the general dirty condition of the boat. The list soon mounts up.

The next thing to decide is whether the boat is to be laid up afloat or slipped and stored for the winter in a cradle on land. Boat owners who never cruise during the winter may opt for the latter which, in my opinion, is the best method. There are four steps in the sequence of events: slipping the boat, laying up, which involves removing everything that can be removed off the boat and protecting that which is left behind, ensuring the boat is set on a stable support on land, and providing coverage from the elements. If the hull needs no repair work or painting, it can be left afloat which will save on hauling out charges, but beware of the possibilities of ice, especially with a glass-fibre boat on a narrow waterway such as a canal where the occasional passing steel-hulled craft might cause great sheets of razor-sharp ice to damage the hull.

The Boat at Home

For those owners with smaller craft and some space to keep them at home, the prospects are of saving money on boat-yard storage and the ability to undertake quite major repair work and engine servicing. A boat on the drive is within reach of all your tools, as well as fresh water, and an electricity supply, which is quite important when using power tools. If you do opt for a boat-yard, make sure that the one chosen is a reputable one with fire, theft and damage insurance which covers craft in their care. If you are having work done by the yard, set firm start and completion dates as many yards are busy during winter and spring. Also, try to get a realistic estimate on the price of the work to be done. Remember, you can save yourself a lot of money by following the procedure laid out here and doing the main jobs yourself. Finally, you should regularly visit your boat throughout the winter or get a friend to check it for you, ensuring the security of the storage cradle and repositioning covers as necessary. Once you have decided where you are going to store the boat, you can then get down to work.

A great deal of damage can be done to a boat's engine over the winter months, more than any amount of normal running during a cruising season. Diesel engines should be run up to temperature while the craft is still afloat. Observe the readings on the oil pressure and temperature gauges to see that all is well. When the engine is hot, pump out the sump oil, using the lift pump attached to the engine or one of the new portable, 12-volt DC oil-change devices, or drain it from the block into an old bowl. Refill through the oil-filler cap with a rustproofing agent, such as Esso Rust Ban 623, or a similar make, then treat the gearbox lubricant in the same way. Turn the engine over gently to spread the lubricant around the oil jacket and check for leaks. Drain off the fuel filter and take off the inlet pipe to the fuel-lift pump. Place this in a small tin containing a mixture of one-third Rust Ban 623 to two-thirds diesel fuel. Bleed off the fuel system and then restart the engine, running at high speed to distribute the protective lubricant around the system.

Filters

Remove and replace all the oil and air-filter elements, not forgetting to change the oil in the oil bath air filters, if fitted. If the engine has a freshwater, 'closed' cooling system, drain this off then use a flushing solution to cleanse the cooling jacket. Add antifreeze in the correct proportion and quantities for your engine. (The details of all lubricants and the capacity of the engine's water system will be found in the handbook.) A good way of telling that the antifreeze has filled the system on a raw-water-cooled engine is to take off the raw water inlet pipe from the sea cock, put the free end of the hose in a bucket holding a solution of antifreeze, then run the engine until the coloured liquid flows from the exhaust. This shows that the antifreeze has passed through all parts of the engine's cooling jacket.

To protect the cylinder walls from rusting during their period of inactivity, carefully take out each injector in turn and tip a teaspoonful of light machine oil into each cylinder. Turn over the engine by hand to distribute the oil over the cylinder walls. If you have a petrol engine, take out each spark plug and do the same thing, replacing each plug with a correctly set new one or cleaning the heads of the old plugs.

The exterior surface of the engine can be cleaned off using a degreasing solution and any chipped paintwork touched up using a hard-wearing enamel paint such as Hammerite. The electrical system, leads to the alternator, starter motor and, on a petrol engine, the distributor leads and cap should be protected from water and condensation by spraying with WD40. Seal off the air intakes on an air-cooled engine with pieces of cardboard to prevent condensation and moisture building up inside the engine. Remove the impeller in the water-circulating pump to prevent it from becoming misshapen inside its housing. It is always a good idea to replace it in the spring. Greased bearings on the alternator and starter motor should be repacked with grease and then sprayed with moisture repellent.

Remove the batteries, take them home and trickle charge them, cleaning the battery casing and smearing some grease on to the terminals. At least once during the winter discharge the battery completely over a period of about 6 hours and then immediately re-charge it. This will help to remove any sulphation from the cell plates and keep the battery in top condition. Top up each cell with distilled water (not water from a fridge as this will be contaminated with grease, etc.) to a level not exceeding a quarter-of-an-inch above the baffle plates, visible through the filling caps. Remember when trickle charging your batteries to do it in a well-ventilated area. This will ensure that any gasses formed by the charging process will be dispelled. The electrolyte (battery fluid) expands with charging, so do not over-fill the cells.

Outboards

Outboard engines are best removed from the boat and taken home where they can be serviced with ease. Secure the engine to a plank on the workbench or on a special outboard stand. An old oil drum, filled three-quarters full with water, will be handy for running the engine off the boat. Take off the top cowl and remove the spark plugs, checking each one for signs of wear at the electrode gaps. If badly pitted, oiled or worn replace with the correct types, setting the gaps. Before replacing the plugs, squirt a teaspoonful of light oil, such as 3 in 1, into each cylinder through the plug hole, then turn over the engine by hand to spread the lubricant over the inside cylinder walls.

Oil Change

This is also a good time to change the gear case oil. Locate the two screws on the lower leg of the engine marked OIL DRAIN and OIL FILL. Take out both screws, reserving the fibre washers. Drain off the old lubricant into an old tin and observe if any water comes out with the oil or if the oil has a milky-white colour. If it does, this could mean that the engine has a faulty gearbox oil seal which will have to be replaced. Inject a tube of fresh outboard gear oil of the appropriate type into the lower FILL hole until oil is seen flowing from the upper DRAIN hole. This will ensure a full gearbox with no trapped air. If you own a four-stroke outboard, change the engine sump oil in the same way, using the correct grade, usually SAE 10W-30 or all-year-round 20-50 motor oil. The capacity of most outboards is around 2 litres.

If possible, drain the carburettor of petrol by opening the drain screw and collecting the fuel in a tin. (Remember to dispose of this in the correct manner!) Check the fuel lines for signs of wear and perishing, tightening clips and connections. If the outboard uses a remote fuel tank, examine the feed pipe and primer bulb for wear, the tank for corrosion, checking the inlet filter at the bottom of the fuel pipe pick-up and apply a little light grease to the connection valve to stop corrosion. It is best to drain integral fuel tanks of petrol or two-stroke mixture as fuel does not like being left for long periods and can deteriorate. It is also a good safety measure, especially if you intend to store the engine in the garage at home.

Basic Lubrication

Apply a light grease to all linkages on the carburettor, throttle and gearchange linkages, swivel bracket and transom clamps. A waterproof grease such as Duckhams Keenol is ideal. An essential part of outboard winterizing is to flush out the engine's cooling jacket with fresh water. This is especially important if the engine is used regularly in salt-water conditions or in areas of high pollution. This can be done in the test tank by running the engine up to temperature, out of gear for about ten minutes. Most modern outboards now come with a special FLUSH attachment comprising a plug, which is inserted into a socket on the lower leg, and which is attached to a hose-pipe, enabling fresh water to be forced around the system.

Take off the propeller and examine the shaft for foreign bodies, such as fishing line, bits of rope and other debris. Remove these or they may damage your seals as well as inhibit the performance of the engine. Grease the propeller shaft and hub, replacing the shear pin as a matter of course. If the propeller is badly damaged with bits missing from the blade tips, send it away for repair to a reputable propeller dealer. If all is in order, replace the propeller and its nut and fit a new cotter pin, finally enclosing the end of the lower leg in a protective canvas bag.

Wash down the exterior of the motor in a mild soapy solution. Touch up any chipped paintwork with an enamel spray of the appropriate colour, replacing worn sacrificial anodes on the lower leg. Before replacing the top cowl, spray over the power head with WD40 waterproofing agent, paying special attention to the electrical and ignition circuits. If possible, store the outboard upright on its own stand in a cool, dry place.

Outdrive Units

Outdrive units need little attention except for checking the rubber boot or bellows that surround the swivel fitting between the engine and the boat. If this boot is perished, worn or split it should be replaced immediately to prevent an ingress of dirt which could soon seize the moving parts. A new one can be purchased by referring to your outdrive handbook, noting down the part number and quoting this along with the model number of the unit when ordering. Change the oil in the gearbox, watching out for those tell-tale signs of water penetration, check the condition of the sacrificial anodes and remove the propeller, examining the shaft for fishing line, etc. Grease the propeller shaft and steering linkages, touching up any chipped paintwork, then surround the leg with a protective cover if the boat is stored on land. If the boat is fitted with a 'sail-drive', where the leg passes through the bottom of the boat near the stern, the rubber sealing flange should be inspected for signs of leaks and replaced, if required.

Electrics

Check the operation of all lights inside the boat; cabin, berth and chart-table lights, replacing bulbs and strip tubes if blown and checking the operation of all switches. Remove switch covers and give the contacts a spray of WD40 to stop corrosion and do the same with bulb holders. Check the fuse panel and main distribution board. Are the fuse terminals free of corrosion and tight? Check your supply of spare fuses, replenishing those values that you have used through the season. Examine visible wiring, clipping up any sagging loops and replacing temporary taped-up joints in cables with proper jointing boxes, sleeving or barrier-strip couplings. On the outside of the cabin, look at the through-the-deck fittings and remove any corrosion on plugs and sockets, greasing terminals and

replacing any broken fittings. Check the operation of all navigation lights, re-placing dud bulbs and spraying bulb holders with protective waterproofing agent. Check that all torches, lifebuoy beacons and spotlights are in a working condition, removing the dry cells before storing. Portable instruments such as radio/cassette players, TVs and video equipment should be taken home, along with any items of navigation equipment that can be easily removed such as the echo sounder, VHF radio and Decca. Place the loose ends of equipment supply cables in plastic bags, securing with an elastic band to stop condensation from attacking the terminals.

Water System

Drain the boat's water system to prevent

Turn off the gas supply to the water heater and isolate the supply of water. Drain down the internal water jacket which will prevent it from splitting in the event of a freeze.

To drain down the water system, remove the inlet pipe from the water tank to the main water pump. This will prevent damage to the pump impeller if the water should freeze. Place the end of the pipe into a plastic bag and seal with an elastic band to keep the inside clean until the spring.

the possibility of frozen pipes and burst water-heater jackets. Before doing this, flush the system through with a mild solution of Milton fluid or proprietary brand of water-tank cleaner. Open all taps and run until the water tank is empty, then take off the outlet pipe from the main water pump, put the loose end in a bucket, and run the pump to purge the inlet piping of water. Leave these pipes disconnected and all taps left open, but make a note to reconnect them in the spring **before** trying to fill the water tank, and tie up all loose pipes or enclose in small plastic bags to prevent contamination. Check the condition of pipe clips, sea cocks and their gate valves, replacing corroded clips and greasing valves where required. Inspect all water pumps, checking seals and 'O' rings on mechanical versions, cleaning switches and checking wiring to electric ones. Turn off the gas supply to the water heater at the isolating tap then drain the system.

If the boat is fitted with a chemical toilet, empty it, flush it out and store off the boat. Pump-out systems with holding tanks should be pumped out, flushed

Remember to turn off all sea cocks and isolate taps before leaving the boat over the winter, especially if it is to be left moored afloat.

through with fresh water and pumped out again. Check all pipework for leaks and corroded clips, closing off any gate valves along the route. Disinfect the toilet seat and surrounding area, cleaning the floor and wiping down surfaces. Sea toilets should be isolated from their inlet and drain pipes at both pump and toilet, draining the pump and flushing out the toilet bowl. Grease the sea cocks and repack glands with grease making sure that they can be turned on and off with ease. Clean out the shower tray and remove and service the shower pump, cleaning out hair and debris from the intake filter. The whole toilet/shower compartment can be washed down with a mild soapy solution and an air freshener left *in situ* over the winter. Shower curtains should be removed and taken home for washing and storage.

Bilges

Take up as many floorboards as you can to gain access to the bilges. Clean these out, removing water and any mud and silt that has found its way in. Poke some thick wire through the limber holes to help clear them if blocked, then dry the bilge area, painting with primer or red oxide paint, if necessary. If the boat is to remain afloat during winter, check that the automatic

119

bilge-pump float switch still works and that the sonic (non-moving) switch is clean and clear of debris. Of course, a battery must be left connected to the pump in this situation, and the pump switch should be left on automatic mode. While in the bilges, examine the stern gear, repacking the gland with grease and giving a couple of turns to ensure good penetration to the tube. If your stern tube is fitted with a clamp-type coupling, make sure that it is tight and does not leak.

Remove all upholstery, curtains and cushions from the boat and store at home in plastic bags. Clean out lockers and generally tidy the cabin, sweeping floors and vacuuming carpets which, if removable, should also be taken off the boat. The galley should be cleaned down, the sink trap cleaned out and the skin fitting closed off to prevent icy draughts. Remove all foodstuffs from cupboards and empty the fridge, washing it out with a solution of bicarbonate of soda. Isolate the cooker from the gas supply and, if possible, take it off the boat for a thorough cleaning. Burners should be removed and checked for rust and blockages, washing them and rinsing off in warm, soapy water. Clean all galley work surfaces with disinfectant (Dettox will do) then leave a small window slightly ajar to keep the air circulating,

The galley should be cleaned down and fridge washed out using a mild solution of bicarbonate of soda. Leave the door slightly ajar to allow air to circulate which will help to prevent mould from forming.

Cupboards and cabins can have small dehumidifiers posted to take out any excess moisture from the air. Don't forget to leave a small window or vent open to allow fresh air to circulate, especially if the boat is to be fitted with a protective tarpaulin or cover.

even if the boat is to be stored under a canvas cover.

Safety Equipment

Remove all dry-powder fire extinguishers and have them checked and serviced by your local dealer. Check the condition of the fire blanket in the galley and that it slips out of its container easily. The flare pack should be checked to see that flares have not passed their use-by date and then taken off the boat and stored in a dry place at home. Send the life-raft, if you have one, for servicing to an authorized service agent and check the operation of the emergency lifebuoy and life-jacket strobe

lights. Do **not** check that your EPIRB satellite rescue location device is working unless you want to initiate a full search and rescue operation. Apart from tying up the emergency services on a fruitless mission, you could land yourself with an enormous bill for services rendered! The contents of the first-aid box should be checked and replenished as required.

Washing Down

Start the wintering procedure on the outside of the boat by hosing down the cabin sides, superstructure and decks with freshwater to help remove salt deposits and to dislodge grime. Scrub the hull to remove barnacles and scrape off any

Stubborn grime, such as this, on the cabin of a glass-fibre narrow boat can usually be cleaned off using a proprietary cleaning agent, a scrubbing brush and plenty of elbow grease. The dirt on this particular boat has built up because its regular mooring spot is under several old trees.

A small, portable power spray is being used to wash off the topsides of a yacht. These high-pressure units can also be used to clean off quite stubborn weed growth from the hull after the boat has been slipped from the water and chocked up on dry land.

attached weed growth. Scrubbing the hull is one of the more unpleasant jobs to do for winter lay-up. Many people leave it until spring, but it is best to get it out of the way before the onset of winter when weed and growth is still relatively soft. The antifouling paint may have built up causing the bottom to be rough, so scrub this down with a coarse sanding block (remembering to wear a mask and keep the working area wet to avoid breathing in poisonous dust), or use a suitable paint stripper. Never burn off antifouling as it will produce deadly toxic fumes. Once scrubbed clean, and after repairing any minor damage (see chapter on GRP repairs), give the hull a coat of primer followed by a coat of the appropriate approved antifouling.

The hull itself should be cleaned down, major and minor repair work carried out

The best method of protecting the boat left unattended afloat for several months is to place several fenders strategically along its length.

and given a good coat of wax polish. Remember not to use a silicone-based wax and do not buff off. Varnish work on hatches, sea rails and around windows should be scraped off, if flaking, and a fresh coat comprising 50 per cent varnish and 50 per cent white spirit painted on. Scrape off flaking paint on straight timber, priming and recoating with a suitable paint system.

Rigging

On a sailing yacht, examine the rigging for signs of wear and fatigue, cleaning and oiling all halyard sheet winches and washing all running rigging in freshwater before dismantling and storing. Wash down stainless steel rigging and store. Galvanized rigging should be washed in freshwater, dried, then soaked in a mixture of petrol and raw linseed oil. This will help to prolong the life of the rigging and keeps corrosion at bay.

Remove all sails, take them home and soak in warm, soapy water remembering not to use any form of detergent. Scrub off staining with a hard-bristled brush and, once dry, repair any tears and relash eyelets and cords, etc. Fold the sails carefully and stow them in their bags in the loft at home.

Once the topsides have been cleaned and any damage to decks and fittings repaired, the winter cover can be fitted. The cover, whilst keeping out all weather, should be fitted to allow a free passage of ventilating air. The cover should be wide enough to cover the topsides of the boat and should be properly secured to prevent flapping in the wind, with lines tied down to the support cradle or to strong spars on the boat itself. The usual method of fitting a cover is to erect a stout timber frame over the topsides and hang the cover over this.

SUMMARY

- Wintering the boat at the end of the useful cruising season is an essential part of boat ownership and will go a long way in keeping the fabric of the boat in good condition. Plan your campaign before you start so that you will have a good idea of work that needs to be done and parts that will need to be purchased.

- It is particularly important to winter the engines aboard. Failure to do so could result in blown core plugs, split cooling pipework and general degradation during winter. The outboard can easily be wintered at home.

- The best way to store the boat over the winter is on dry land on a special support frame with a canvas or tarpaulin cover mounted on a frame. Remember to allow a free flow of fresh air to the boat cabin by leaving a couple of small windows open.

GLOSSARY

Accelerator One of the two compounds (the other is catalyst) required to initiate the polymerization process. (*See* Pre-accelerated.) Mixed directly with catalyst, accelerator acts explosively and is therefore usually added to the resin in manufacture so only the catalyst component needs to be added later.

Acetone Solvent for cleaning uncured resin from brushes and tools. It is highly inflammable and a powerful grease solvent which should **not** be used for removing resin from the skin where it will destroy the natural oils and can lead to dermatitis.

Aerosil An extremely lightweight filler powder, so light that is likely to become airborne if not dispensed with care. It is used to thicken resins and make them thixotropic.

Air inhibition Air inhibits the curing process in some resins, with the result that the exposed resin surface tends to remain tacky. This effect is used deliberately in gel coats, but can be a problem with some resins. Some additives designed to prevent air inhibition can discolour resins.

Binder In chopped strand mat (the most commonly used glass fibre material), the strands are held together in a random pattern by a binder, either a PVA emulsion or a polyester powder. Powder-bound mat gives faster wet-out but emulsion-bound gives greater ease of handling.

Brush cleaner A solvent for uncured resin, based on recycled acetone. It is highly inflammable.

Carbon Fibre An extremely strong reinforcement which can be used in conjunction with glass fibre and resin.

Catalyst This can also be called hardener and is a special compound which, when mixed with an accelerator, starts the polymerization or curing process of polyester and other resins. It should never be mixed directly with accelerator as this could cause an explosion! Catalyst is available as a liquid or paste. Catalyst is a powerful corrosive and should not come into contact with eyes, mouth or skin. Should it do so, wash from the skin with fresh running water. If splashed in the eyes, flush them with running water for fifteen minutes, and seek medical advice.

Catalyst dispenser A purpose-designed instrument for measuring and dispensing liquid catalyst without splashing.

Chopped strands Short 6mm (¼in) or 12mm (½in) lengths of glass fibre which is used to make a resin 'dough', stronger than that made by mixing resin with filler powder.

Chopped strand mat A popular and economical form of glass reinforcement used with polyester resins. Short strands of glass are bonded with a powder or emulsion into a mat which can be bought in a variety of thicknesses.

Cold curing Able to cure to a hardened state at room temperature, usually when activated by a catalyst.

Compressive strength The ability of a material to withstand being crushed. It is found by testing a sample to failure, the load applied, divided by the cross-section of the sample, gives the compressive strength.

Contact moulding Any method of moulding glass fibres without external pressure, as is used in injection moulding. The commonest contact methods are hand lay-up and spray moulding.

Consolidating Using a metal roller on a glass fibre and resin layer to force out air bubbles.

Cure Normal term for the polymerization process by which the polyester resins harden.

Curing agents Chemicals used to initiate the polymerization process in resins, for example the catalyst or accelerator.

Curing time The period required for polyester resin to cure fully. In practice it is taken as the time from the addition of the catalyst to the point of full hardening. A resin may actually continue to cure for some time after it is apparently completely hard.

Epoxy Resin sometimes used for glass-fibre work, having good adhesive properties, but is slightly more difficult to use and is far less popular than polyester resins.

Exotherm The internal heat generated within a resin by hardening process. As the resin cures it becomes noticeably hotter.

Female mould A mould in which the internal surface decides the form of the casting or laminate taken from it. A child

using a bucket to make sand castles is using a female mould. *See* Moulds.

Filler Any substance added to a resin to extend it. A typical filler is an inert calcite (talc) which increases the bulk of the resin without affecting its chemical properties. Most fillers have the advantage of reducing exotherm.

Finishing Glass-fibre materials, once hardened, can be polished, sanded, drilled, sawn or filled. Diamond carborundum or metal finishing tools are generally required. Since the dust produced can be extremely hazardous to eyes and lungs, protective goggles and breathing masks should be worn at all times when machining hardened resins, with or without glass-fibre reinforcement.

Former Anything around which GRP lamination can be laid, e.g. a cardboard tube can be used as a former for a laminated rib. The term is also used for the 'pattern' or 'plug' from which a mould is taken.

Furane Resin often used on a plug, especially a wooden plug, to give a highly glazed surface.

Gel Before hardening completely, a catalyzed resin first reaches a thick, jelly-like consistency known as the gel state. Once it reaches this stage, the resin is impossible to spray, paint or pour. Stored resin which has passed its shelf life may gel without being catalyzed.

Gel coat A thixotropic resin invariably used as the first coat (applied without glass reinforcement) on the surface of the mould. It forms the hard, smooth shiny surface of the finished article and is usually pigmented. It will paint on easily but does not drain from vertical surfaces.

Gel time The period between a resin catalyzing and reaching gel state, in effect,

GLOSSARY

the time in which it is still workable. Gel time varies from one type of resin to another and is also known as the setting time.

Glass fibre Glass filaments drawn together into fibres and used to reinforce polyester resins, to produce a strong, lightweight, versatile material. The fibres can be woven into a variety of fabric types or used as a random matrix of short, chopped strands held together by a powder or emulsion binder.

GRP Abbreviation for Glass-fibre Reinforced Plastic. The plastic is invariably a resin, sometimes epoxy but usually polyester.

'Green' stage A point reached by a GRP laminate after the gel time but before it is fully hardened. While 'green', the laminate is fairly firm but can be cut with a knife and is easy to trim at this stage.

Hand lay-up The process of applying the resin and glass laminate to the mould manually with brushes and rollers. A cheap but effective method, requiring no specialized equipment and therefore the most popular DIY method.

Hardener *See* Catalyst.

Inhibitor Any substance which slows or stops the curing process. Air is an inhibitor to the surface of some resins, oil and water will inhibit most.

Kerocleanse A proprietary cleansing cream which removes resin, etc., from the skin. It is rubbed in prior to washing in soap and water.

Kerodex A proprietary barrier cream which helps to protect the skin against polyester resins, etc. If not washed off, an application is effective for two to three hours.

Laminate Any material in which separate layers of material are bonded together. In GRP work, the layers are resin and glass fibre. Polyester resins can be laminated with cloth, felt or paper in certain applications.

Lay-up The process of applying the resin/glass laminate in the mould. *See* Hand lay-up and Spray lay-up.

Male mould A mould having the external working surface onto which the laminate is laid up.

Maturing time The time taken for an apparently hardened resin to become completely cured and stable. This is important when making moulds and in certain specialized applications.

MEKP Metal Ethyl Ketone Peroxide, an organic peroxide and the main constituent of a widely used catalyst for polyester resin.

Melinex A plastic polyester film which does not adhere to resin, and therefore can be used for self-releasing formers.

Moulds Many glass-fibre projects require a mould in which to cast the resin and lay up the laminations. A mould can be made of almost any material as long as it is sufficiently rigid, has a smooth surface, and will not adhere to the resin (or can be treated so that it will not do so). The most usual mould materials for laminating are wood or GRP. Moulds can be male or female, with the lamination being applied to the exterior of a male mould and the interior of a female one.

Paddle roller A type of metal roller used in laminating.

Parting agent *See* Release Agent.

Paper rope Paper wound on a wire core and used as a former, over which to laminate stiffening ribs, etc.

Pattern *See* Plug.

Pigments Conventional polyester resins are translucent and cloudy and can be coloured with the addition of a wide variety of pigments which can be opaque, translucent or metallic.

Plasticizer An additive which increases the flexibility of resins.

Plug Also known as a pattern or former, a plug is a full size mock-up from which a mould is taken. The mould is then used to produce the finished glass-fibre article.

Polyester A substance produced by reacting certain glycols (alcohols) with anhydrides (organic acids). Conventional GRP resins are polyesters dissolved in styrene.

Polyethylene Commonly called poly-thene, as it is completely resistant to polyester resins it can be used for buckets, mixing containers and small casting moulds. Polythene sheeting can be a useful releasing agent in some circum-stances.

Polystyrene Polyester resins attack and dissolve polystyrene, which cannot there-fore be used for storage containers, etc.

Post cure The application of heat to accelerate the complete curing process and shorten maturing time.

Pot life The working time of a resin, the period between the resin being catalyzed and becoming gelled.

PVA The abbreviation for Polyvinal Alcohol which is a substance used as the basis of some release agents.

Release agent Since polyester resins adhere to most substances to some extent (with the exception of a few plastics) moulds invariably have to be treated to enable the finished laminate to be released easily. This treatment usually takes the form of polishing with purpose-designed

waxes called release agents. Moulds made of polypropylene, polythene, or silicone rubber will be self-releasing, as will those protected by a sheet of polythene or Melinex film.

Resins These substances occur naturally as organic compounds which are soluble in organic solvents but not in water. Synthetic resins have similar properties and are normally produced by polymer-ization. The resins most used in GRP are polyesters.

Resin stripper Used for removing hard-ened resin from brushes and tools. It is extremely caustic and should never be allowed to come into contact with skin, eyes or mouth.

Respirator Breathing mask incorpor-ating filter designed to protect the lungs from minute particles of dust and/or harmful fumes. It is essential when sanding down glass-fibre laminates.

Rollers See Laminating Tools.

Rovings Long fibres of glass held together by dressing, supplied in a 'cheese'.

Sheathing The process by which an item is given a protective skin of resin-impregnated glass fibre and is often applied to boat hulls.

Shelf Life Catalysts and accelerators speed up the polymerization process, but even without these additives resins will tend to polymerize slowly by themselves. Because of this, all resins have a shelf life which is normally from three months to one year depending upon the type of resin and the storage facilities.

Spray lay-up Mainly used in large boat building workshops, spray lay-up is a process which involves spraying the resin, catalyst and chopped glass fibres into the mould from a special spray gun.

INDEX